MASTER CLASS

AT JOHNSON & WALES

Cuisinart
SAVOR THE GOOD LIFE™

weber

Cascade

MASTER CLASS

AT JOHNSON & WALES

Recipes from the Public Television Series

Produced by Marjorie Poore Productions

Photography by Alec Fatalevich

⁂ TABLE OF CONTENTS

✦ INTRODUCTION

For almost 30 years, the professional chefs at Johnson & Wales University have been teaching students from all across the country, indeed all over the world, the art and science of preparing wonderful food – the techniques, the cuisines, the cornerstones of the profession and the creative touches that are the hallmark of a true culinary professional. And now, through the public television series, "Master Class at Johnson & Wales" and this, the first companion cookbook, we are able to bring the opportunity to participate with our chefs and students to you – home cooks and food lovers, amateur and professional alike.

In this cookbook you will find recipes that we have developed in response to the trends and interests that are relevant to today's fast-paced and global society. The cuisines of many different nations are represented here – often "translated" for the modern cook, who more and more often is looking for a recipe with high nutritional value without sacrificing great taste. From Apple Crisp French Toast to Southwestern Zucchini, it's all here. Whether your taste runs to new twists on old favorites, like Chicken Wellington or you want to take a culinary tour of Asia and aren't afraid to take on Crying Tiger, you'll find recipes to intrigue and delight. We've even dedicated an entire section to healthy cuisine.

Chef-instructors from all of our campuses, from the original campus in Providence, Rhode Island to our newest location in Denver, Colorado, participated in the show and the book, providing our students with yet another opportunity for the hands-on learning that is a hallmark of a Johnson & Wales education. In some cases the students themselves provided recipes and direction – creating original dishes or new twists on old standards. The dynamic relationship between our chefs and students is unique to the Johnson & Wales experience, and we hope it has been translated to the television screen and the printed page in the form of these master classes.

We also invited a group of distinguished guest chefs – some alumni and some former visiting lecturers – to prepare some of the recipes that they have made famous in their own varied careers. This included a master class with chef Paul Bocuse at the CuisinArt Resort and Spa in Anguilla, where a select group of students from our groundbreaking bachelor's degree program in culinary nutrition created an assortment of delectable and nutritious recipes using fresh ingredients from the resort's hydroponic farm.

So if you've watched the show and have seen the chefs and students demonstrate their baking expertise or their mastery of the sauté pan, now you can follow along with the clear and concise, step-by-step instructions found in this book.

The public television show, "Master Class at Johnson & Wales" and this companion cookbook will be, for some of you, the welcoming of an old friend into your living room and your kitchen. For others, it will be your first introduction to Johnson & Wales. Either way, we are confident that you will savor some wonderful new tastes, discover recipes destined to make it into your family favorites, and find inspiration for your own culinary adventures, all without leaving the comfort of home!

⤳ ACKNOWLEDGMENTS

Johnson & Wales University – America's Career University" is a private, non-profit educational institution with campuses in Providence, Rhode Island; Norfolk, Virginia; Charleston, South Carolina; North Miami, Florida and Denver Colorado. With associate and bachelor's degree programs in our College of Culinary Arts in culinary arts, baking and pastry arts, and culinary nutrition, as well as foodservice management degrees housed in The Hospitality College, we are the world's largest foodservice educator.

We would like to thank a number of individuals and companies whose contributions to "Master Class" made it possible to bring Johnson & Wale's unique brand of culinary education to people all across the country.

We're very proud to have Cuisinart as our sponsor. The company, which created a culinary revolution in the early 70's when they brought the first food processor from France to the U.S., is a true leader and innovator in the field of small kitchen appliances. It's been a genuine pleasure to work with their many fine products, not to mention their supportive staff. A special thank you to its owner Lee Rizzuto who made it possible for us to film Paul Bocuse at the beautiful CuisinArt Resort and has been such a great supporter of Master Class. We'd also like to thank Mary Rodgers for her many contributions to this project and for all the hard work and long hours she devoted to it.

We are also delighted to have the Weber-Stephen Products Co. as a supporter and sponsor of the series. They have set the standards for grilling in this country, offering home cooks the highest quality equipment which makes grilling a genuine pleasure. Our chefs have thoroughly enjoyed using their grills and are grateful to have them at Johnson & Wales. A big thank you to Mike Kempster, Sr. for all his personal efforts and contributions to the series.

One of the first things a chef learns is the importance of cleanliness in the kitchen. Therefore, we're tremendously pleased to have the support of the company which is regarded as the most famous and reliable name in the world of household cleaning, Procter & Gamble and its brand Cascade. For decades, the company has revolutionized products that aid every busy kitchen, whether professional or in the home. Our gratitude extends to their wonderful staff, a "shining" example of creative talent led by Marketing Director, Kristen Nostrand and Brand Manager, Lela Coffey.

We also must thank the talented team at Marjorie Poore Productions. Led by Producer/Director Marjorie Poore and Executive Producer Alec Fatalevich, their creative talents and dedication to finding a way to bring the essence of a Johnson & Wales education to the television screen were inspirational to the administrators, chefs and students who participated in this project.

Our distinguished guest chefs, who took time from their own busy careers to work with us, added a whole new dimension to the show, as did the staff at the CuisinArt Resort and Spa in Anguilla.

Linda Beaulieu, the talented editor of this book, and the dedicated and ever-questioning group of recipe testers, ensured that the creations of the classroom were appropriate for the "typical" home cook in his or her kitchen.

Special thanks to University President John Yena and Providence Campus President John Bowen '77, who made sure we had what we needed to get the job done, and the J&W team who worked diligently and happily to bring this project to fruition: Steven Shipley, Piya Sarawgi, Judith Johnson, Miriam Weinstein and the many others who worked with them behind the scenes.

The chefs and students of Johnson & Wales University were the true stars of the show, and their work both on and off-camera will be forever appreciated.

Karl Guggenmos
Dean – College of Culinary Arts
Johnson & Wales University

Chef Instructors

Adrian Barber
Elena Clement
John Dion
Kevin Duffy
Christian Finck
Karl Guggenmos
Andrew Hoxie
Dean Lavornia
Diane Madsen
Kim Gibbs-O'Hayer
George O'Palenick
Harry Jo Peemoeller
Joseph Peter Reinhart
Steven Shipley
Frank Terranova
Martin Tuck
Patricia Wilson

Distinguished Guest Chefs

Dr. Noel Cullen, C.M.C.
Dr. Madeleine Kamman
Paul Bocuse
Daniel Bruce
Ulrika Bengtsson
Peter Cooper
George Germon
Denis Jaricot
Johanne Killeen
Daniel Orr
Guy R. Reinbold
Randy Waidner

Students

Andrea Ainbinder
Laurie Anderson
Anthony Audette
Kurt Batchelder
Kyle Blais
Karen Breen
Gloria Maria Cabral
Katie Carroll
Daniel Marc Coward
Charlie Cummings
Katherine Dent
Jessica Emery
Karen Fernandez
Kerry Fisher
Gregory Javonillo
Elizabeth Kamien
Kathryn Lamberson
Emily LaRose
Charlene Lucca
Jane A. Matanguihan
Rich Montalvo
Timothy McGinnis
Kari Naegler
Michael Sabrin
Chuck Schestak
Varun Shivdasani
Edward Sheets
Jeffrey Squires
Yean Hoong Teh
Francis Toher
Lucille White

CARIBBEAN

→ JAMAICAN JERK CHICKEN WITH COCONUT RICE AND RED PEAS

Jamaican jerk seasoning is a dry seasoning blend that originated on the Caribbean island of Jamaica. Used primarily in the preparation of grilled meat, it is usually a combination of chiles, thyme, cinnamon, ginger, allspice, cloves, garlic and onions. In Jamaica all beans and peas are called peas. So when people talk of rice and peas, they really mean rice and red kidney beans.

1 tablespoon allspice
1 fresh red chili pepper, seeded and finely chopped
2 scallions, thinly sliced
6 chicken leg quarters
¼ cup soy sauce
2 tablespoons dark rum
Salt and freshly ground black pepper, to taste

2 cups coconut milk
2 scallions, chopped
2 sprigs fresh thyme, finely chopped
1 garlic clove, minced
1 small sweet pepper, finely chopped
Salt and freshly ground black pepper, to taste
2 cups long-grain white rice

To make the jerk rub:

In a bowl, combine the allspice with the chili pepper and scallions. Rub this mixture all over the chicken. Place the chicken in a large baking dish. Allow to stand at room temperature for 10 minutes.

In a small bowl, combine the soy sauce and dark rum. Pour this mixture over the chicken. Cover and refrigerate for 1 to 2 hours.

To cook the chicken:

Prepare a grill or preheat oven to 400 degrees.

The chicken may be grilled or roasted in a preheated 400-degree oven for 30 to 40 minutes. Season to taste with salt and pepper. Serve with Coconut Rice and Red Peas (recipe follows).

6 SERVINGS

Coconut Rice and Red Peas

1 cup dry red kidney beans (or you may use canned beans)
4 cups boiling water

To prepare the red kidney beans:

Place the dry beans in a large bowl, cover with cold water and soak overnight. On the following day, drain and rinse well.

Place the beans in a large pot and add the boiling water. Cook for about 30 minutes or until almost tender. Add the coconut milk, scallions, thyme, garlic and sweet pepper. Season with salt and pepper. Bring to a boil again, and cook for 3 to 5 minutes.

Add the rice and stir well. Cover and simmer gently over low heat until the rice is tender and the liquid has been absorbed, approximately 25 to 30 minutes. Transfer to a serving dish and serve hot.

✴ **CHEF'S NOTE:** If you use canned beans, cook the rice, coconut milk, scallions, thyme, garlic and sweet pepper in the 4 cups of boiling water until the rice is tender and the liquid has been absorbed, 25 to 30 minutes. While the rice is cooking, drain and rinse the canned beans. During the last 5 minutes of cooking, fold in the beans, stirring gently.

6 SERVINGS

✦ CURRIED SHRIMP AND PINEAPPLE OVER STEAMED RICE WITH MANGO AND PAPAYA CHUTNEY

Curry comes from the southern Indian word kari, meaning sauce, which is a term that is used to refer to many hot, spicy, gravy-based dishes of East Indian origin. Curry powder is a key ingredient in all curries.

1 and ¹/₂ pounds raw shrimp, peeled and deveined

Juice of 1 lime

2 tablespoons vegetable oil

1 medium-size yellow onion, finely chopped

1 garlic clove, finely chopped

1 tablespoon finely chopped chives

2 tablespoons curry powder

1 cup fish stock, canned clam juice or water

Salt and freshly ground black pepper, to taste

2 tablespoons arrowroot

2 tablespoons water

1 (20-ounce) can pineapple chunks, drained

To prepare the shrimp:

Sprinkle the shrimp with the lime juice. Set aside.

In a saucepan, heat the oil over medium-high heat. Add the onions, garlic, chives and half of the curry powder. Cook for 5 minutes or until onions are soft. Add the shrimp and the remaining curry powder. Cook for about 3 minutes. Add the fish stock or water. Bring to a boil. Reduce heat to a simmer. Season with salt and pepper.

In a small bowl, combine the arrowroot and water. Add this mixture to the curried shrimp. Add the pineapple. Simmer for 5 minutes. Serve the curried shrimp over plain steamed rice with mango and papaya chutney (recipe follows).

6 SERVINGS

Mango and Papaya Chutney

2 cups under-ripe diced mangoes

2 cups under-ripe diced papaya

¹/₂ cup raisins

2 hot diced peppers

4 cups malt vinegar

4 cups sugar

¹/₂ cup ground ginger

2 garlic cloves

¹/₂ pound onions, chopped

Salt, to taste

To make the chutney:

In a large saucepan, combine the fruit and peppers with the vinegar, and allow to steep until the next day. Add the sugar, ginger, garlic, onions and salt. Over medium-high heat, bring to a boil; reduce heat and simmer until chutney is thick and brown. Makes about 2 cups.

ITALY

→ SMOKED CHICKEN AND GOAT CHEESE SPINACH MANICOTTI WITH ROASTED TOMATO AND PORTABELLO MUSHROOM BUTTER SAUCE

This recipe calls upon the cook to use a smoker to smoke chicken breasts. If you do not have a smoker, smoked chicken or smoked turkey can be purchased in the deli department of large supermarkets.

Honey Brine:
1 gallon water

3/4 cup kosher salt

1 cup sugar

2 teaspoons whole cloves

2 teaspoons freshly ground black pepper

1/2 cup honey

Chicken Stuffing:
1 pound chicken breasts, skinless and boneless

1/3 cup shredded goat cheese

1/2 cup ricotta cheese

1/3 cup heavy cream

2 eggs

2 sun-dried tomatoes, chopped and soaked in sherry wine

1 tablespoon chopped fresh basil

Oil, as needed

1 cup diced onions

1 cup diced zucchini

1/2 cup diced mushrooms

1/2 cup grated Parmesan cheese

Pasta Dough:
3 eggs

1 tablespoon olive oil

1/4 cup cooked spinach, squeezed dry

2 cups all-purpose flour

Salt, to taste

Optional: 1 tablespoon water, if needed to hold dough together

To make the honey brine:
In a large saucepan, combine all the brine ingredients over high heat. Bring to a boil. Reduce to a simmer. Cook for 20 minutes. This makes enough to brine a whole chicken.

To make the chicken stuffing:
Soak the chicken breasts in the honey brine overnight. Using a smoker, smoke the chicken over wood chips until the chicken has an internal temperature of 160 degrees on a meat thermometer. Allow to cool.

Dice the chicken by hand, then grind it in a food processor. Add the remaining stuffing ingredients. Blend well. Adjust the seasoning, if desired.

Heat the oil in a large sauté pan. Sweat the onions, zucchini and mushrooms until wilted. Allow to cool. Fold into chicken mixture.

To make the pasta dough and assemble the dish:
In a food processor, combine the eggs, oil and spinach. Blend well. Add flour and salt. Mix until mixture crumbles. Transfer mixture onto a clean floured work surface. Knead dough by hand until the dough is very smooth, 5 to 10 minutes. Wrap in plastic wrap. Allow dough to rest for 10 minutes.

Preheat the oven to 350 degrees.

Roll the pasta dough through a pasta machine, according to the manufacturer's directions. Cut dough into 6x6-inch squares. Place approximately $1/2$ cup of filling into the center of each pasta square. Roll the pasta square into a cylinder to form a manicotti. Place the manicotti in a shallow oiled baking dish. Top the manicotti with Parmesan cheese. Bake for 20 to 25 minutes.

✳ CHEF'S NOTE: Cover the manicotti with aluminum foil if it begins to dry out in the oven. To shred the goat cheese easily, place it in the freezer for 1 hour before grating.

Roasted Tomato and Portabello Mushroom Butter Sauce

3 plum tomatoes

Olive oil, as needed

Garlic pepper, as needed

3 shallots, finely diced

3 portabello mushrooms, washed and diced

1 cup chicken stock

1 cup heavy cream

$1/4$ cup butter

Salt and freshly ground black pepper, to taste

To prepare the tomatoes for roasting:
Preheat the oven to 250 degrees.

Cut the plum tomatoes into 1/4-inch thick slices. Brush the tomatoes with olive oil, and season with garlic pepper. Place the tomatoes on a rack over a sheet tray. Slowly roast the tomatoes for 3 hours.

To make the sauce:
In a saucepan, heat 1 tablespoon olive oil and sauté first the shallots, then the mushrooms until wilted. Add the chicken stock and heavy cream. Bring to a boil and reduce by half.

Remove the pan from the heat. Cut the butter into small pieces. Add the butter a piece at a time to the simmering chicken stock, until each piece is completely melted. Add the mushrooms and tomatoes to the sauce. Season to taste with salt and pepper. Simmer for 5 minutes. Serve over the manicotti.

✳ CHEF'S NOTE: If you don't have time to roast the plum tomatoes for the sauce, you can use sun-dried tomatoes, available in the gourmet section of most supermarkets.

→ GRILLED EGGPLANT BUNDLES

The most common eggplant is the large, pear-shape variety with a smooth, glossy, dark purple skin. It's available year-round, with the peak season during August and September. Choose a firm, smooth-skinned eggplant heavy for its size. Avoid those with soft or brown spots.

2 large eggplants, skin removed

Olive oil, as needed

Salt and freshly ground black pepper, to taste

½ pound fresh ricotta

½ pound fresh mozzarella, chopped

¼ cup diced plum tomatoes

1 teaspoon chopped fresh thyme

2 tablespoons chopped fresh basil

1 tablespoon olive oil

1 teaspoon minced garlic

Sauce:

¼ cup olive oil

3 garlic cloves, minced

1 and ½ cups chopped plum tomatoes

1 tablespoon chopped Italian parsley

1 tablespoon chopped fresh basil

Salt and freshly ground black pepper, to taste

To grill the eggplant:

Prepare the grill.

Slice the eggplants lengthwise into 1/4-inch thick pieces. Lightly brush the slices with olive oil. Season with salt and pepper. Quickly grill the slices on both sides over medium-high heat, about 30 seconds per side. Remove from the heat. Allow to cool.

To make the filling:

In a large bowl, combine the ricotta, mozzarella, tomatoes, thyme, basil, oil and garlic. Season to taste with salt and pepper. Spread a small amount of this mixture on each slice of eggplant. Roll up and secure with a toothpick. Refrigerate.

Once again, prepare the grill. Over medium-high heat, grill the eggplant bundles, carefully turning them to cook until heated through. Keep warm.

To make the sauce:

In a saucepan over medium heat, combine the oil and garlic. Sauté for 2 minutes, then add the tomatoes, parsley, basil, salt and pepper. Heat for 2 minutes. Remove the toothpicks from the eggplant bundles. Place the bundles on a serving plate and top with the sauce. Serve at once.

✳ **CHEF'S NOTE:** Soak the toothpicks in water for at least 30 minutes so that they won't burn when placed on the grill.

4 SERVINGS

→ ARRAGOSTA ALLA GRIGLIA CON COCO E ZENZERO (GRILLED LOBSTER WITH COCONUT AND GINGER)

The Asian flavors of coconut milk, sesame oil, ginger and lime make this an unforgettable lobster dish.

1 tablespoon sesame oil

2 tablespoons minced onion

2 scallions, minced

1 tablespoon curry powder

1 cup canned coconut milk

1 tablespoon minced fresh ginger

1 and ½ tablespoons fresh lime juice

3 kaffir lime leaves

⅛ teaspoon cayenne pepper

Salt, to taste

4 lobster tails (North Atlantic variety), split in half

To make the coconut sauce:

In a saucepan, heat the sesame oil. When hot, add the onions, scallions and curry powder. Sauté for 2 to 3 minutes until the curry is fragrant. Add the coconut milk and ginger. Simmer for 10 minutes. Add the lime juice, lime leaves and cayenne pepper. Season to taste with salt. Strain and set aside.

To grill the lobsters:

Prepare the grill.

Place the lobsters on the grill, shell side down, and baste them heavily with the coconut sauce. After 3 minutes, turn over the lobsters and move them to the cooler side of the grill. Close the lid to the grill to cook the lobsters for another 3 minutes, or until the lobster shell is bright red and the lobster meat turns white. Open the lid to the grill, and once again turn over the lobsters so they are shell side down again. Baste with the coconut sauce. Remove the lobsters from the heat and place them on a serving platter. Drizzle any remaining coconut sauce on the lobsters. Serve at once.

✳ **CHEF'S NOTE:** Imported from Southeast Asia and Hawaii, the glossy, dark green kaffir lime leaves used in cooking have a unique double shape and look like two leaves that are joined end to end. Fresh and dried kaffir lime leaves can be found in Asian markets. The fresh leaves have a more intense, fragrant aroma.

4 SERVINGS

→ PANÉ SICILIANO (SEMOLINA BREAD)

This dough requires a large percentage of prefermented dough to create a fabulous interior crumb. The semolina flour adds a golden hue and sweet, nutty characteristic, but it is a very hard wheat that does not lend itself to an open texture. Combining prefermented dough and overnight fermentation helps you achieve results rarely seen even in Sicily.

1 pound pâte fermentée (recipe follows)

2 and ¼ cups high-gluten bread flour

2 and ¼ cups semolina flour

2 teaspoons table or sea salt

2 teaspoons instant yeast or 2 teaspoons active dry yeast

1 tablespoon sugar

1 tablespoon olive oil

1 and ¾ cups water, lukewarm

Garnish: 2 tablespoons sesame or black sesame seeds for the tops

To make the bread:

Make the pâte fermentée (prefermented dough) the day before and chill it overnight.

One hour before making the Pané Siciliano, take the prefermented dough out of the refrigerator, cut it into about 10 pieces, cover it with a towel, and let it come to room temperature.

In a mixing bowl, combine all the ingredients, including the prefermented dough pieces. If using active dry yeast, dissolve it first in 1/4 cup of the water for about 3 minutes before adding it to the dough. Stir the ingredients until they form a ball of dough.

Sprinkle some flour on a clean counter and transfer the dough to the counter. Knead by hand for about 12 minutes, adding flour or water to make a smooth, soft, supple, tacky but not sticky dough. If using an electric mixer, mix for about 4 minutes on medium slow speed. Let the dough relax for 5 minutes, then mix again for 3 to 4 minutes, adjusting flour or water as described above. In a food processor, mix for 45 seconds, wait 5 minutes, then mix for 45 additional seconds, using the metal blade, not the plastic blade.

Transfer the dough to a bowl that has been lightly oiled, roll the dough to coat it with oil, and cover the bowl with plastic wrap. Let the dough rise at room temperature for approximately 90 minutes, or until doubled in size.

Carefully transfer the dough to the counter. Divide the dough into 3 equal pieces with a serrated knife or a pastry blade, being careful not to degas the dough any more than necessary. Gently form the dough into 24-inch baguette lengths. Coil the dough, spiraling it from each end toward the center, like an "S" (or cut the dough into smaller pieces and make rolls of any shape or size).

Place the three "S" shaped pieces on one or two sheet pans that have been covered with baking parchment and dusted with semolina flour. Mist the tops of the breads with water and sprinkle the sesame seeds over the tops. Spray the dough with vegetable oil spray and slip the pan(s) into a large plastic bag and place in the refrigerator overnight.

The next day, check the dough to see if it has doubled in size. If not, remove the pan(s) from the refrigerator and allow about 2 hours for the yeast to wake up and for the dough to continue rising. The dough should be plump and will hold a dimple when poked with a finger, rather than spring back.

Place a pan containing 2 cups of hot water in the oven on a different shelf than where you plan to bake.

Preheat the oven to 500 degrees.

When the oven is ready, place the pan(s) on the middle shelf and spray the oven wall with water from a mister. Wait 30 seconds and repeat this spraying. Repeat once more after another 30 seconds.

Reduce the oven temperature to 450 degrees and bake for 10 minutes. Then, rotate the pans 180 degrees and continue baking for approximately 10 to 15 minutes, or until the bread is a rich golden brown all around. When the bread appears done, turn off the oven and wait 5 minutes, then remove the bread from the oven, and transfer it to a cooling rack. Wait at least 1 hour before eating.

MAKES 3 LOAVES OR MANY ROLLS

Pâte Fermentée (Prefermented Dough)

2 and $^1/_2$ cups high-gluten bread flour

1 teaspoon table or sea salt

1 teaspoon instant yeast (or 1 teaspoon active dry yeast dissolved in $^1/_4$ cup warm water)

$^1/_2$ to 1 cup water, at room temperature

In a mixing bowl, combine all the ingredients together, using only $^1/_2$ cup of water at first. Stir everything together until the ingredients form a ball of dough. Drizzle in more water if needed.

Sprinkle some flour on the counter, transfer the dough to the counter and knead it by hand for about 10 minutes. Add flour or water as necessary to make a smooth, supple, tacky but not sticky ball of dough.

Lightly oil a bowl and roll the dough in the bowl to coat it. Cover the bowl with plastic wrap and let the dough rise for about 45 minutes. It should increase by about 1 and $^1/_2$ times in size. Take the dough out of the bowl and knead it for a few seconds to de-gas it. Form it back into a ball and return it to the bowl, again covering it. Immediately place the bowl in the refrigerator overnight. Makes about 1 pound of prefermented dough.

→ CHICKEN LEGS STUFFED WITH PANCETTA AND CHEESE

Pancetta is an Italian bacon that is cured with salt and spices but not smoked. Flavorful and slightly salty, pancetta comes in a sausage-like roll and is used in Italian cooking to flavor sauces, pasta dishes, vegetables and meats. Pancetta should be tightly wrapped and refrigerated for up to three weeks, or frozen for up to six months.

6 chicken legs (drumsticks and thighs)

$1/4$ pound pancetta, thinly sliced

2 ounces fontina cheese

1 garlic clove, minced

3 sage leaves, minced

1 fresh rosemary sprig, minced

1 tablespoon butter

3 tablespoons olive oil

$1/2$ cup sherry wine

Salt and freshly ground black pepper, to taste

1 tablespoon cornstarch

1/4 cup heavy cream

2 to 3 tablespoons tomato sauce

To prepare the chicken:

Clean and rinse the chicken legs. Remove the bones without cutting into the chicken legs by working the flesh down the bones, removing the bones, and pushing the legs back into shape. (You may want to ask your butcher to do this for you.)

Mince the pancetta. Cut the fontina cheese into tiny cubes. In a bowl. combine the pancetta and cheese with the minced garlic, sage and rosemary leaves. Stuff the chicken legs with this mixture, sewing the openings shut with a needle and thread.

In a very large sauté pan, heat the butter and oil. Brown the chicken on all sides. Sprinkle the sherry wine over the chicken. As soon as the sherry wine has evaporated, season the chicken with salt and pepper. Dust the chicken with the cornstarch.

Add the cream and tomato sauce to the pan, stirring to keep lumps from forming. Reduce the heat to low and simmer for 40 minutes, stirring in more liquid (water or low-sodium chicken broth) if necessary. The chicken should be quite tender and the sauce pleasingly thick.

6 SERVINGS

→ FETTUCCINE WITH MASCARPONE AND PARMIGIANO-REGGIANO

This is a delicate dish with a silky sauce that clings to the fettuccine. The pepper adds a counterpoint to the texture and taste, while the parmigiano-reggiano adds a luxurious note.

2 large eggs

3 tablespoons mascarpone cheese

$1/2$ teaspoon kosher salt plus extra for the pasta water

12 to 18 turns of the peppermill

$1/2$ cup parmigiano-reggiano cheese plus a little extra for garnish

8 ounces imported dried fettuccine

To begin cooking the pasta:

Bring 6 quarts of water to a boil in a large pot. Add 3 tablespoons kosher salt to the boiling water.

To make the sauce:

While the water is coming to a boil, whisk the eggs, mascarpone, $1/2$ teaspoon salt, pepper and parmigiano-reggiano in a heat-proof mixing bowl. Set aside.

To finish cooking the pasta:

Drop the fettucine into the pot of boiling water and cook at a full rolling boil, stirring frequently, until al dente, 5 to 7 minutes. While the pasta is cooking, rest the mixing bowl above the boiling water to warm the mixture. Stir frequently to prevent the eggs from curdling. When the fettucine is al dente, drain and toss the pasta into the mascarpone mixture. Sprinkle with additional cheese, toss well, and serve immemdiately.

✳ **CHEF'S NOTE:** Buy fettuccine packaged in nests rather than flat. The flat strands of fettuccine tend to stick together in the boiling water no matter how much you stir.

4 SERVINGS AS A FIRST COUSE OR

2 SERVINGS AS A MAIN COURSE

✦ PAPPARDELLE WITH OLIVES, THYME AND LEMON

In this dish, the saltiness of the olives plays remarkably well against the pungency of fresh thyme. Citrus peel is added for a bright note, and the red pepper flakes contribute a little zip.

3 and $^1/_2$ tablespoons kosher salt

16 calamata olives, pitted

Zest of 1 lemon, coarsely chopped

1 (3-inch) strip of orange peel, coarsely chopped

$^1/_4$ teaspoon crushed red pepper flakes

1 tablespoon fresh thyme leaves

$^1/_2$ cup fresh Italian flat-leaf parsley

$^1/_2$ teaspoon kosher salt

2 tablespoons extra virgin olive oil

8 ounces dried imported pappardelle

To begin cooking the pasta:

Bring 6 quarts of water to a boil in a large pot. Add the kosher salt.

To make the sauce:

While the water is coming to a boil, combine all the ingredients, except the pappardelle, in the bowl of a food processor. Pulse on and off until you have a chunky puree. Transfer to a warm serving bowl large enough to accommodate the cooked pappardelle. Set aside in a warm place.

To finish cooking the pasta:

Drop the pappardelle into the pot of boiling water. Cook at a full rolling boil, stirring frequently, until the pasta is al dente, 5 to 7 minutes. Drain the pappardelle, reserving 1 cup of the cooking water. Toss the pasta into the serving bowl with the olive mixture. Add 1/4 cup of the cooking liquid and toss well. Add more liquid if needed. Pappardelle has a tendency to absorb liquid quickly so you may need to add more water. The sauce should cling to the ribbons of pasta but should not be dry. Serve immediately.

4 TO 6 SERVINGS AS A FIRST COURSE, OR 2 SERVINGS AS A MAIN COURSE

→ SPAGHETTI ALLA CHITARRA WITH POTATOES, GORGONZOLA AND SAGE

Pasta and potatoes may seem like an odd combination, but the two are joined together in several dishes from Tuscany. Red Bliss potatoes are recommended for their creamy texture, but russets or Yukon gold potatoes may also be used. Gorgonzola cheese and sage round out this dish. Fresh, not dried, sage should be used.

2 small Red Bliss potatoes, peeled and cut into
  ¹/₂-inch pieces
3 tablespoons unsalted butter, cut into small dice
2 tablespoons crumbled Gorgonzola cheese
1 scant tablespoon finely minced fresh sage
3 and ¹/₂ tablespoons kosher salt
8 ounces imported spaghetti alla chitarra*
5 or 6 turns of a peppermill

To prepare the potatoes:
Combine the cubed potatoes and at least 6 quarts of water in a large pot. Bring to a rapid boil and cook the potatoes for 5 minutes.

To make the sauce:
Meanwhile, with a fork, mash the butter, cheese and sage together in a serving bowl large enough to accommodate the cooked pasta. Set aside in a warm place.

To cook the pasta:
After the potatoes have boiled for 5 minutes, add the kosher salt to the water and drop in the spaghetti. Cook at a full rolling boil until the pasta is al dente, 5 to 6 minutes. Drain the pasta and potatoes in a colander, reserving about ¹/₂ cup of the cooking water.

Transfer the pasta and potatoes to the serving bowl. Gently toss with the butter and cheese mix-ture. Add freshly ground pepper and 1/4 cup of the pasta water. Toss again. Add more water if necessary. The sauce should be glossy with the consistency of heavy cream. Serve immediately.

4 SERVINGS AS A FIRST COURES OR 2 SERVINGS AS A MAIN COURSE

*Available in specialty markets or you may substitue linguini or spaghetti

✦ PLUM CROSTATA

Crostata is a rustic open-face or lattice-top Italian tart. Pasta frolla, meaning "short pastry," is made with a high amount of fat.

Pasta Frolla (Dough):

2 and ½ cups plus 2 tablespoons all-purpose flour

½ cup plus 2 tablespoons unsalted butter, at room temperature, cut into chunks

½ cup plus 2 tablespoons granulated sugar

3 large egg yolks

Plum Filling:

8 fresh plums, pitted and sliced

2 tablespoons granulated sugar

½ cup orange marmalade

2 tablespoons Grand Marnier or orange liqueur

To make the pasta frolla:

In the bowl of a food processor, combine the dough ingredients and pulse until the dough comes together. Shape the dough into a disk. Wrap in plastic wrap and chill the dough, approximately 15 to 20 minutes.

To assemble the crostata:

Preheat oven to 375 degrees.

Remove the dough from the refrigerator, and allow it to come to room temperature. On a floured surface, roll out the dough to make a 12- to 14-inch circle. Transfer the circle of dough to a large parchment-lined pan or cookie sheet.

Beginning in the center of the tart, fan the sliced plums on the dough in a decorative pattern, leaving an outside edge of 3 inches of dough. Fold this outer edge of the dough over the outer plums. Most of the plums in the center of the tart will be exposed. Sprinkle the tart with granulated sugar and bake for about 22 to 25 minutes, or until golden brown.

In a small saucepan, bring the marmalade and liqueur to a boil, and pour over the tart. Allow to cool. Cut and serve.

8 SERVINGS

EASTERN EUROPE

✈ SAUTÉED CHICKEN BREAST WITH A WILD MUSHROOM CRUST AND GRILLED BELL PEPPERS WITH PAPRIKA CREAM

Paprika is a powder made by grinding sweet red pepper pods. The flavor ranges from mild to pungent and hot. Most commercial paprika comes from Spain, South America, California and Hungary. The Hungarian variety is considered superior. All supermarkets carry mild paprikas, while ethnic markets have the more pungent varieties.

Wild Mushroom Crust:

1/2 cup dried wild mushrooms

1 cup fresh bread crumbs

1 tablespoon paprika (sweet or hot)

2 tablespoons garlic pepper

Paprika Cream:

4 tablespoons whole grain mustard

2 egg whites

4 chicken breasts

1/4 cup olive oil

1 cup finely diced onions

1/2 cup sliced shiitake mushrooms

1 tablespoon paprika (sweet or hot)

1/3 cup sherry wine

2 cups heavy cream

To coat the chicken:

Place the dried mushrooms in a food processor and grind them into a powder. In a large mixing bowl, combine the mushrooms, bread crumbs, paprika and garlic pepper.

In a small mixing bowl, blend the mustard and egg whites. Coat the chicken breasts completely with the mustard mixture. Dredge the chicken breasts in the mushroom powder, making sure to coat them evenly.

Preheat oven to 350 degrees.

In a non-stick sauté pan, heat the oil and brown the chicken on both sides. Place the chicken on a sheet pan and bake at 350 degrees for 15 to 20 minutes or until the chicken has an internal temperature of 160 degrees on a meat thermometer.

To make the paprika cream:

Add more oil to the sauté pan if necessary, and sauté the onions and shiitake mushrooms until wilted. Dust the onions and mushrooms with paprika.

Deglaze the pan with sherry wine, and reduce the mixture by one-half. Add the heavy cream, and reduce until thickened. Adjust the seasoning, if desired.

Serve this paprika cream with the chicken and grilled bell peppers (recipe follows).

4 servings

→ GRILLED BELL PEPPERS

Marinade:

¹/₂ *cup oyster sauce*

¹/₄ *cup sherry vinegar*

¹/₄ *cup granulated sugar*

¹/₂ *teaspoon red pepper flakes*

¹/₂ *cup white wine*

¹/₄ *cup olive oil*

¹/₂ *red pepper*

¹/₂ *yellow pepper*

¹/₂ *green pepper*

¹/₂ *orange pepper*

1 *red onion, cut into* ¹/₄-*inch thick rings*

To make the marinade:

Combine all the marinade ingredients in a stainless steel bowl. Blend well.

To prepare the peppers:

Wash the peppers, and remove all seeds. Cut the peppers into large pieces. Add the cut-up peppers to the marinade along with the onion rings. Allow to marinate for 3 hours at room temperature.

Preheat the grill. Grill the peppers and onions until tender but still firm to the bite. Cut the peppers into thin julienne strips and serve along with the onions.

→ CRANBERRY APPLE ROLL

The old practice of encasing various fillings in this delicious dough is truly characteristic of Russia. This dessert utilizes available ingredients and is shaped in the traditional rectangle referred to in Russian as the "pirogi" which is derived from "pir" meaning feast. The pirogi is integral to Russian-style entertaining.

Filling:

1 cup cranberries

¹/₂ cup sugar

2 tablespoons honey

1 tablespoon water

Zest from ¹/₂ lemon

2 tablespoons flour

¹/₄ teaspoon cinnamon

2 large tart apples, finely chopped

Pastry:

¹/₂ cup butter, softened (1 stick)

4 ounces cream cheese, at room temperature

1 yolk

1 and ¹/₂ cups flour

¹/₄ teaspoon salt

To make the filling:
In a medium-size saucepan over high heat, combine all the filling ingredients, except the apples, and bring to a boil. Simmer until the cranberries burst open. Remove from heat. Fold in chopped apples. Set aside. Cool completely.

To make the pastry:
Blend together the butter and cream cheese. Add the egg yolk, mixing well. Slowly add the flour and salt until completely incorporated.

Preheat oven to 375 degrees.

On a lightly floured surface, roll out the dough to approximately 9x18 inches. Place the filling down the middle of the dough. Fold the dough on the right over the filling, and fold the dough on the left over that, sealing all the edges. Place the roll seam side down on a baking sheet. Using a fork or sharp knife, pierce holes in the dough along the top of the roll. Brush with an egg wash, if desired.

Refrigerate the roll for 1 hour before baking.

Bake for about 1 hour. Allow to cool slightly before serving.

CHEF'S NOTE: A lattice-type finish to this roll is optional.

10 SERVINGS

GREECE

→ GRILLED BUTTERFLIED LEG OF LAMB

In the past, lamb was known as a special occasion meat, but new breeding techniques have lowered prices. A leg of lamb can be bought, boned and butterflied to cut down the cooking time.

Marinade:

4 garlic cloves, peeled

2 teaspoons dried Greek oregano

2 tablespoons fresh rosemary leaves

$1/2$ teaspoon freshly ground black pepper

$1/4$ cup brown sugar

$1/2$ cup olive oil

$1/4$ cup fresh lemon juice

$1/4$ cup white wine

3-pound butterflied boneless leg of lamb, 1 and $1/2$ inches thick

To prepare the marinade:

In a food processor, combine the garlic, oregano, rosemary, pepper and sugar. Pulse to chop coarsely. Add the oil, lemon juice and white wine. Pulse to combine. Pour mixture into a shallow glass or ceramic dish.

Place the lamb in the marinade for at least 3 hours or overnight, turning the lamb twice during that time.

Preheat the grill to medium-high heat.

To make the glaze:

Transfer the lamb to a plate. Transfer the marinade to a saucepan, and reduce by half over medium heat. Set aside.

Place the lamb on the grill to cook with direct heat for 10 to 12 minutes per side, with the grill cover closed. Continue cooking until a meat thermometer inserted into the thickest part of the lamb reads 140 degrees. During the last 2 minutes of grilling, baste both sides with the glaze.

To serve the lamb:

Transfer the lamb to a cutting board. Allow to rest for 5 minutes. Slice across the grain and serve with Tzatziki (recipe follows).

4 SERVINGS

⊹ TZATZIKI

Tzatziki is a traditional Greek dipping sauce made with Greek yogurt which is very thick and dense. The coolness of the cucumber and yogurt balances the tangy flavor of the grilled lamb. If unavailable, use regular plain yogurt which you should drain through cheesecloth to achieve a similar product. Tzatziki can be served as a dip with pita bread, raw vegetables, grilled meat kebabs and tabbouleh salad.

16 ounces plain yogurt
1 cucumber, peeled, seeded and grated
2 garlic cloves, minced
1/2 teaspoon minced chili pepper
1 tablespoon finely chopped fresh dill
2 tablespoons extra virgin olive oil
1 tablespoon red wine vinegar
Salt and freshly ground black pepper, to taste

Empty the yogurt into a double layer of cheesecloth. Tie securely and allow the yogurt to drip for 2 hours into a small bowl. After 2 hours, place this "yogurt cheese" in a clean mixing bowl.

Cut the cucumber in half and grate in a food processor. Squeeze the grated cucumber in cheesecloth to remove excess moisture. Combine the cucumber with the yogurt cheese. Mix in the garlic, chili pepper, dill, oil, vinegar, salt and pepper. Refrigerate until needed.

4 SERVINGS

GRILLED FIGS WITH YOGURT CHEESE, HONEY AND ORANGE FLOWER WATER

If fresh figs are not available, fresh white peaches would make a great alternative. Orange flower water adds the aroma of orange blossoms to desserts and pastries. It is very popular throughout the Mediterranean and now can be found in American supermarkets.

1 quart plain low-fat yogurt
¹/₄ cup honey
2 teaspoons orange blossom water
8 ripe purple figs, cut in half lengthwise
¹/₄ cup shelled pistachios, toasted and chopped

Making the yogurt cheese:

Empty the yogurt into a double layer of cheese-cloth. Tie securely and allow the yogurt to drip for 2 hours into a small bowl. After 2 hours, place this "yogurt cheese" into a clean mixing bowl. Cover and refrigerate until needed.

Making the honey syrup:

In a small saucepan, heat the honey and orange blossom water. Remove pan from heat.

Grilling the figs:

Preheat the grill. Spray the figs with olive oil spray, and place the figs on the grill directly over the heat. Grill for 3 to 4 minutes on each side, or until the figs begin to soften in texture. The cooking time depends on how ripe the figs are. The riper the fig, the quicker it will cook. With a pastry brush, brush the cut sides of the figs with some of the honey syrup mixture. Grill the figs cut side down for 1 more minute, allowing the honey to caramelize.

Serving the grilled figs and yogurt cheese:

On each dessert plate, place a large dollop of fresh yogurt cheese. Drizzle the remaining honey syrup over the yogurt. Place 4 fig halves on top and sprinkle with toasted pistachios. Garnish with orange blossoms, a mint sprig or a sprig of lavender, if desired. Serve immediately.

✳ **CHEF'S NOTE:** If orange blossom water is not available, you may substitute 1 tablespoon orange zest. Leftover yogurt cheese can be refrigerated and used as a dipping sauce with raw vegetables.

4 SERVINGS

→ MARINATED FETA CHEESE, ROASTED PEPPERS, OLIVES AND WILD ARUGULA SALAD

Greek food is fresh, delicious, simple to prepare, and healthy. This recipe encompasses the flavors of Greece and makes a nice accompaniment for grilled lamb or chicken.

2 red bell peppers

2 garlic cloves, minced

2 tablespoons red wine vinegar

2 tablespoons honey

1/2 cup extra virgin olive oil

1 pound feta cheese, cut into 1/2-inch cubes

1 cup Greek kalamata olives, pitted

1 cup red onion, sliced 1/8-inch thick

1 tablespoon chopped fresh mint

2 bunches wild arugula, washed and dried

1/2 teaspoon freshly ground black pepper

Roasting the peppers:

Place the peppers on a hot grill as close to the flame as possible, and grill until the skin begins to blister and turn black on all sides. Remove the peppers from the grill. Cover the peppers with plastic wrap to allow the skins to soften. When the peppers are cool enough to handle, peel off the charred skin. Remove the seeds and cut the peppers into large strips.

Making the dressing:

In a small bowl, whisk together the garlic, vinegar, honey and olive oil. Set aside.

Assembling the salad:

In a large bowl, combine the peppers, feta cheese, olives, onions and about half of the dressing. Marinate for 1 hour to mingle flavors and soften textures. Just before serving, toss with mint and arugula. Serve the remaining dressing on the side.

✳ **CHEF'S NOTE:** If you are unable to find wild arugula, baby field greens may be substituted.

4 SERVINGS

THAILAND

⊹ CHU-CHI GOONG

Many of the ingredients in this recipe can be found in Asian markets, but a surprising number are also now available in the international aisle of large American supermarkets.

Chu-Chi Paste:

1 teaspoon sea salt

6 garlic cloves, minced

1 tablespoon minced cilantro

1 dried poblano (or ancho) chili, softened in warm water

15 dried chilies, softened in warm water

1 tablespoon dried shrimp, softened in warm water*

1/2 teaspoon Thai white peppercorns, dry roasted and ground*

1/2 teaspoon caraway seeds, dry roasted and ground

1 teaspoon minced fresh ginger

1 stalk lemon grass, trimmed and minced

1 teaspoon grated lime zest

2 shallots, minced

1 tablespoon grated coconut

1 teaspoon fermented shrimp paste*

Chu-Chi Shrimp:

1 and 1/2 pounds large shrimp, peeled and deveined

Sea salt, as needed

2 cups vegetable oil

2 cups plus 2 tablespoons unsweetened coconut cream*

1/2 cup Chu-Chi Paste (see preceding recipe)

2 tablespoons fish sauce*

2 tablespoons brown sugar

Garnish:

6 serrano chilies, cut into thin julienne strips

15 mint leaves, cut into thin julienne strips

1/4 cup cilantro leaves, cut into thin julienne strips

To make the paste:

Using a small food processor, grind the salt and garlic into a coarse paste. Add the cilantro, chilies, dried shrimp, peppercorns, caraway seeds, ginger, lemon grass, lime zest and shallots. Grind into a smooth paste. Stir in the grated coconut and shrimp paste. Transfer to a bowl, cover and refrigerate.

To prepare the shrimp:

Sprinkle shrimp with sea salt. Place in colander and drain for 10 minutes. Rinse with cold water and dry thoroughly with paper towels.

In a deep pan, heat the oil to 325 degrees. Deep-fry the shrimp for 1 minute; remove and set aside.

In another large skillet, combine the coconut cream with the Chu-Chi Paste. Place over high heat, stirring until it reaches a simmer. Lower heat, and cook until it thickens, about 7 minutes. Add the shrimp and increase heat to high. Add the fish sauce and brown sugar; cook to reduce slightly.

Transfer shrimp to a serving plate. Garnish with serrano chilies, mint leaves and cilantro leaves. Serve with Thai jasmine rice.

*Available in Asian markets.

6 SERVINGS

❖ SEUR RONG HAI (CRYING TIGER)

Not for the faint of heart, this recipe calls for lots of garlic and 2 to 3 serrano chili peppers, but add more if you like it hot, hot, hot!

2 teaspoons dried green peppercorns*
1 tablespoon Big Four Paste (recipe follows)
10 garlic cloves, lightly crushed
2-3 serrano chilies, minced (or more to taste)
1 pound chicken breast, boneless and skinless
1/4 cup vegetable oil
Water, as needed
1 teaspoon fish sauce*
1 tablespoon sugar
2 tablespoons coarsely ground pork rinds*
20 cilantro sprigs, chopped coarsely

To make the glaze:

In a large skillet, dry roast the peppercorns over medium heat for about 2 minutes. Remove from heat. Allow to cool.

Combine the Big Four Paste and garlic in a food processor. Blend until the mixture becomes a well-blended paste. Add the chilies and pulse the processor for 15 additional seconds. Set paste aside.

To prepare the chicken:

Cut the chicken breasts into strips.

Return the large skillet containing the peppercorns to high heat for 2 minutes. Add the oil and paste mixture, stirring quickly for 2 minutes. Add the chicken pieces, lower the heat, and add a small amount of water to prevent the paste from burning. When the chicken is browned on both sides, reduce heat. Add the fish sauce and sugar to the center of the skillet. Bring to a simmer. Reduce until the chicken is evenly coated with the glaze. Transfer chicken to serving plate. Garnish with ground pork rinds and cilantro.

Big Four Paste
1 tablespoon coriander seeds
2 tablespoons Thai white peppercorns*
1 teaspoon sea salt
12 to 15 garlic cloves
1 cup minced cilantro stems

Grind all the ingredients in a small food processor. Store in a covered container in the refrigerator.

*Available in Asian markets.

2 SERVINGS

KOREA

✦ GRILLED PORK STEAKS

This dish is very spicy and can be made fiery hot with additional bean paste and/or cayenne pepper.

1 pound pork loin, cut into 4 steaks

2 tablespoons hot bean paste

1 teaspoon cayenne pepper

1 tablespoon soy sauce

2 teaspoons sesame oil

4 garlic cloves, minced

1-inch piece ginger, peeled and minced

1 tablespoon sugar

Preparing the meat:

Combine all the ingredients, except the pork. Score the steaks deeply and spread the paste mixture over both sides of the steaks. Allow to stand at room temperature for about 30 minutes.

Grilling the steaks:

Preheat the grill to high heat. Oil the grill well. Place the steaks on the grill and cook them quickly, using direct heat and turning them often to prevent burning.

Serving the steaks:

If desired, cut the pork steaks into thin strips. Serve with steamed rice and an assortment of Asian condiments such as, vinegar dipping sauce, sesame oil or soy sauce. May be accompanied by lettuce leaves in which to roll the pork.

✳ **CHEF'S NOTE:** To make the pork loin easier to slice, first place it in the freezer for about 45 minutes, then slice.

4 SERVINGS

❖ BEEF AND GREEN ONION SAN JUCK

San Juck is the Korean name normally given to foods placed on skewers. The assembled skewers may be grilled or deep fried. If using bamboo skewers, it's important to soak them in water for at least 20 minutes before using so they won't burn.

1 pound top round of beef

15 scallions, cut into 3-inch lengths

½ cup soy sauce

¼ cup water

1 tablespoon dry sherry

1 tablespoon sesame oil

1 teaspoon sugar

4 garlic cloves, minced

1 tablespoon sesame seeds, toasted and crushed

Freshly ground black pepper, to taste

Preparing the meat:

Slice the beef into strips approximately 3 inches long and ½-inch thick. Thread the beef onto bamboo skewers which have been soaked in water, alternating each piece of meat with a piece of scallion. Each skewer should hold at least 4 pieces of beef.

Place the skewered beef in a glass bowl large enough to accommodate all the skewers. Combine the remaining ingredients and pour over the skewers. Allow to marinate for about 1 hour at room temperature.

Grilling the skewers:

Preheat the grill to high heat. Oil the grill well. Place the skewers on the grill and cook them quickly, using direct heat and turning them often so they don't burn.

Serving the skewers:

Serve with steamed rice and an assortment of Asian condiments such as vinegar dipping sauce, sesame oil or soy sauce. May be accompanied by lettuce leaves in which to roll the beef.

✳ **CHEF'S NOTE:** To make the eye of the round easier to slice, first place it in the freezer for about 45 minutes, then slice.

4 SERVINGS

✦ SPINACH NA MOOL

Na mool is a marinated or pickled vegetable dish that accompanies Korean meals. Healthy and easy to make, it can also give an asian flair to something as simple as broiled chicken or fish.

1 pound fresh spinach, stems removed
1 tablespoon soy sauce
1 teaspoon sesame oil
1/2 teaspoon sugar
1 teaspoon sesame seeds, toasted

Preparing the spinach:
Wash the spinach and place in microwave-safe bowl. Cover the bowl and microwave for about 30 seconds, or until just limp. Rinse with cold water, drain, and squeeze dry.

Making the na mool:
Combine the remaining ingredients and pour over the spinach.

Serving the na mool:
Serve either at room temperature or chilled as an accompaniment to meat or fish entrees.

4 SERVINGS

⊹ GRILLED SWEET POTATOES WITH SESAME VINEGAR DIPPING SAUCE

Grilled sweet potatoes are wonderful. This dish is a nice contrast to all those sweet potato recipes using brown sugar and butter.

4 sweet potatoes, each about 2 inches wide

2 tablespoons peanut oil

Dipping Sauce:

2 tablespoons water

2 tablespoons soy sauce

1 tablespoon rice wine vinegar

1 teaspoon sesame oil

1 teaspoon sugar

2 scallions, minced

1 tablespoon sesame seeds, toasted and ground

Preparing the sweet potatoes:

Scrub the potatoes well but leave skins intact. Dry the potatoes and punch holes into each with a fork. Rub the potatoes with a little oil. Place potatoes on a hot grill, using indirect heat and turning the potatoes occasionally. Cook for approximately 40 minutes or until soft when pierced with a sharp knife or skewer.

Preparing the dipping sauce:

Combine the remaining ingredients. Divide into 4 individual serving dishes.

Serving the grilled sweet potatoes:

When the potatoes are done, allow them to cool slightly before slicing. Serve with the dipping sauce.

✳ **CHEF'S NOTE:** To save time, cook the sweet potatoes in a microwave oven before placing them on the grill.

4 SERVINGS

✦ SPRINGTIME KIM CHI

Kim chi is said to be the national dish of Korea as some variety of these pickled vegetables accompanies almost every meal. Although these preserved and fermented recipes traditionally require long preparation times, this recipe is an example of a quick dish more suited to Western tastes.

1 head Chinese cabbage, cut into 1-inch squares

1 cup daikon (Japanese radish), shredded

2 tablespoons salt

6 green onions, sliced

6 garlic cloves, minced

2 tablespoons fresh ginger, minced

1 teaspoon cayenne pepper

6 cups water

2 teaspoons salt

1 tablespoon sugar

Preparing the vegetables:
Combine the cabbage and daikon. Sprinkle with 2 tablespoons salt and mix well. Allow to stand for 30 minutes at room temperature. Place the mixture in a colander and rinse well. Drain.

Making the salad:
Combine the cabbage mixture with the remaining ingredients. Mix well. Allow to stand at room temperature for 2 hours.

Serving the kim chi:
Drain off excess water and serve at room temperature or chilled as an accompaniment to almost any meal.

8 SERVINGS

FRANCE

⇥ COQUILLES A LA MODERN WITH DUCHESSE POTATOES

These tender poached scallops and mushrooms can be served in individual scallop shells or baked in a mashed potato ring. They are finished with a white wine-cheese sauce, topped with grated cheese and broiled golden brown.

¹/₂ cup clarified butter

¹/₄ cup shallots

³/₄ pound bay scallops

³/₄ pound large shrimp (26 to 30 per pound), peeled and deveined

All-purpose flour, as needed

¹/₄ cup dry white wine

³/₄ cup heavy cream

6 button mushrooms, stems removed, quartered and sautéed in butter

2 ounces Swiss cheese, grated

2 ounces Parmesan cheese, grated

Preparing the seafood mixture:

In a sauté pan over medium heat, warm the butter. Add the shallots and sauté gently. Dust the scallops and shrimp in flour. Add the seafood to the sauté pan; cook gently (do not brown). Remove the seafood from the pan. Add the wine to the pan and reduce by half. Slowly add the heavy cream; stir and reduce by half. Using a slotted spoon, return the seafood to the pan. Add the mushrooms to the pan and simmer for 15 seconds. Sprinkle with the grated Swiss cheese.

Plating the seafood mixture:

Preheat oven to 350 degrees.

Place the warm seafood mixture into large scallop shells or a casserole, or inside a border of Duchesse potatoes (recipe follows). Sprinkle with the Parmesan cheese and bake for approximately 15 to 20 minutes, or place under the broiler until golden brown.

Duchesse Potatoes

2 pounds potatoes, peeled and diced (hold in cold water)

1 tablespoon salt

2 egg yolks (pasteurized, if available)

1 tablespoon melted butter

Ground nutmeg, to taste

Salt, to taste

White pepper, to taste

To prepare the potatoes:

Drain the potatoes being held in cold water. Place the potatoes in a large saucepan with 1 tablespoon of salt and cover with cold water. Bring to a boil, and cook the potatoes until fork tender.

When the potatoes are done, drain and air dry. Place the potatoes in a large mixing bowl. With a hand mixer, combine the potatoes, egg yolks, butter and nutmeg. (Nutmeg has a very strong flavor so be careful that you don't add too much.) Season to taste with salt and white pepper. Allow to cool.

Transfer the cooled potatoes to a pastry bag with a star tip. Pipe the potatoes onto an oven-proof plate in a circle or oval in which the seafood mixture may be placed.

✶ **CHEF'S NOTE:** Clarified butter, also known as drawn butter, is unsalted butter that has been slowly melted to separate the milk solids (which sink to the bottom of the pan) from the golden liquid on the surface. After any foam is skimmed off the top, the clear butter is poured off the milky residue for use in cooking. Because the milk solids have been removed, clarified butter has a higher smoke point than regular butter and may be used to cook at higher temperatures. On the down side, this also means that the clarified butter will not have as rich a flavor.

6 SERVINGS

☆ CHICKEN WELLINGTON

Beef Wellington is a classic dish. In this recipe, chicken is used instead of beef. The skinless breast of chicken is seared, topped with a mushroom duxelle, encased in flaky puff pastry, baked and served with a mushroom supreme sauce. This main course recipe can easily be adapted to make a miniature version of Chicken Wellington to serve as hors d'oeuvres.

4 boneless, skinless chicken breasts
1 tablespoon clarified butter or oil

Duxelle:
¼ cup clarified butter, heated
¼ cup shallots, minced fine in a food processor
1 cup mushrooms, brushed clean, stems removed and chopped fine in a food processor
1 tablespoon tomato paste
Salt and freshly ground black pepper, to taste

Mushroom Supreme Sauce:
2 tablespoons clarified butter, melted
2 tablespoons flour
1 and ³/4 cups chicken broth, heated
½ cup heavy cream
1 cup mushrooms, brushed clean, stems removed, sliced and sautéed
Salt and freshly ground black pepper, to taste

4 puff pastry sheets, thawed (keep covered and chilled)
Egg wash (egg yolk or egg white mixed with a small amount of water or milk)
4 individual mushrooms, brushed clean with stems remove, for fluting

To prepare the chicken breasts:
In a large frying pan, sear the chicken breasts in the butter or oil. Remove from the pan and refrigerate.

To make the duxelle:
In a saucepan, heat the clarified butter. Add the shallots and cook over medium-high heat until translucent. Add the finely chopped mushrooms. Simmer until the ingredients are almost dry. Add the tomato paste; cook on low heat until fully incorporated. Season with salt and black pepper.

To make the sauce:
In a medium-size saucepan, heat the clarified butter, being careful that it does not turn brown. Add the flour, mixing well. Cook until the mixture has the aroma of toasted nuts. Gradually add the hot chicken broth, mixing well to avoid lumps. Gradually add the heavy cream. Add the sautéed mushroom slices. Season to taste with salt and black pepper.

To assemble Chicken Wellington:
Preheat oven to 400 degrees.

On a clean work surface, lay out the puff pastry sheets one at a time. Place the duxelle on the pastry. Place the cooked chicken breast, best side down, on the duxelle. Brush the pastry with egg wash. Encase the chicken by folding the pastry sheets inward and over the chicken (as in making an egg roll). Or, if desired, the puff pastry sheets can be cut into a cross shape, saving the excess pastry for decorative pieces. Refrigerate (these can be made 3 hours in advance).

Place the puff pastry bundles seam side down on a parchment paper-lined baking pan. Decorate as desired. Brush with egg wash. Bake until an internal temperature of 165 degrees is reached, approximately 20 minutes. Allow to rest; keep warm.

Place a few spoonfuls of sauce on each serving plate. Cut each Chicken Wellington in half on an angle. Place the Chicken Wellington on the plate. Garnish each serving with fluted mushrooms. Serve with roasted potatoes and steamed asparagus.

CHEF'S NOTE: Clarified butter, also known as drawn butter, is unsalted butter that has been slowly melted to separate the milk solids (which sink to the bottom of the pan) from the golden liquid on the surface. After any foam is skimmed off the top, the clear butter is poured off the milky residue for use in cooking. Because the milk solids have been removed, clarified butter has a higher smoke point than regular butter and may be used to cook at higher temperatures. On the down side, this also means that the clarified butter will not have as rich a flavor.

4 SERVINGS

→ CAIEUX À LA CRÈME
(MUSSELS IN CIDER AND CRÈME FRAÎCHE BROTH)

This recipe utilizes some of the most prized products of Normandy, France: large wild mussels going by the local name of caïeux, shallots, dry cider, chives, parsley and crème fraîche. The large cultivated mussels of Maine, preferably from October through April, are perfect for this dish.

2 quarts large Maine mussels

3 quarts cold water

2 tablespoons fine sea salt

1/4 cup unsalted butter, as needed

5 large shallots, chopped very finely

1 large bouquet garni (parsley stems, 1 small bay leaf and 3 sprigs thyme)

1 cup dry hard cider (unsweetened) or very dry white wine of your choice (Muscadet, for example)

1 ounce Calvados or Apple Jack

1 cup crème fraîche

Salt and freshly ground black pepper, to taste

2 tablespoons finely chopped chives

1 loaf light rye bread, sliced

Unsalted butter, as needed

To prepare the mussels:

Place the mussels in a large glass or stainless steel bowl.

In another large stainless steel or glass bowl, prepare a solution of cold water and sea salt, stirring until the salt is completely dissolved. Pour the solution over the mussels and let stand no longer then 20 minutes, stirring occasionally. Discard any mussel that may still be floating after 20 minutes. Drain the shellfish into a colander. Do not rinse.

In a large stockpot, heat the butter and sauté the shallots until they start to turn golden brown.

Add the bouquet garni, cider and Calvados. Bring to a boil, turn down to a simmer, and add the mussels. Cover and steam for 1 minute. Shake the contents of the pan, continue cooking another minute, and shake again. Keep covered while cooking for a total of no more than 4 minutes. The mussels should all be open and still be tender. Do not let them boil. Discard any unopened mussels.

To make the crème fraîche broth and serve the mussels:
Using a slotted spoon, move the mussels to individual serving plates. Blend the crème fraîche into the cooking juices and reheat well without boiling. Season with salt and pepper. Strain the sauce over the mussels and top with chives.

Serve with slices of light rye bread (preferably old-fashioned Jewish rye) and very fresh unsalted butter.

With this soup, serve the same cider or wine used to prepare the dish.

✻ **CHEF'S NOTE:** Fine sea salt is used here because it is easy to find in any supermarket, and it purges pollutants from the mussels which have remained closed since they were removed from their birth waters. Mussels that remain open or that are closed but floating after soaking in the salt bath must be discarded.

6 SERVINGS AS A FIRST COURSE

✦ PATTES DE POULETS AUX PETITS ARTICHAUTS, PETITS POIS ET CITRON (CHICKEN LEGS WITH BABY ARTICHOKES, PEAS AND LEMON)

The dream of "a chicken in the pot of every French family" became a possibility at the end of the 16th century. The upper classes enjoyed the famous "suprêmes" or white meat fillets, while working class women who were employed by the nobility as fine cooks carefully prepared the legs for the household employees who relished those less noble, but oh so much tastier parts of the birds.

6 very large chicken legs

Fine sea salt, as needed

Freshly ground black pepper

3 dozen small whole baby artichokes, about 1 and ¹/₂ inches in diameter

Juice of 1 lemon

2 to 3 cups chicken broth

1 whole lemon sliced into ¹/₄ -inch slices, then chopped and blanched for 3 minutes in boiling water

2 tablespoons unsalted butter

1 cup freshly cooked baby green peas or defrosted baby peas rinsed under hot water

¹/₄ cup crème fraîche (available in most supermarkets)

2 teaspoons each chopped mint, tarragon and chervil leaves

To broil the chicken legs:

Preheat the oven to broil.

Place the chicken legs on a very lightly oiled broiling pan. Broil each side of the legs for approximately 8 minutes. Season the legs with salt and pepper. Lower the rack and continue broiling for approximately 8 minutes on each side until the chicken is golden. Transfer the legs to a sauté pan. You can at this point stop the cooking and finish the dish later if it is helpful to you.

To prepare the baby artichokes:

Remove the stems and outer leaves of the artichokes, and trim them into corklike shapes. Bring a large pot of water to a boil. Add the juice of the whole lemon, the artichokes, salt and pepper, and cook for 5 minutes. Drain and refresh under running cold water. Add the artichokes to the pan containing the chicken. Cook over medium heat for another 20 to 25 minutes, adding chicken broth at regular intervals until you have added at least 1 and ¹/₄ cups. During the last 5 minutes of cooking, add the chopped blanched lemon.

The chicken should be done to the point where a skewer inserted at the center part of the largest leg comes out freely. When the legs are done, add the butter and baby peas, and reheat completely.

Arrange the chicken and its vegetable garnish on a presentation platter. Keep warm and lightly covered.

To make the sauce:

Add another half cup of chicken broth to the emptied pan and reduce to 2 tablespoons on high heat. Turn the heat off, whisk in the crème fraîche, and finally add the fresh herbs. Spoon the sauce over the chicken pieces. Serve promptly.

✳ **CHEF'S NOTE:** The best chicken stock is the one you can make yourself using the carcasses, wings, necks and gizzards of two chickens.

✧ TARTE TATIN

Tarte Tatin is a famous French upside-down apple tart. While baking, the sugar and butter turn into a delicious caramel that becomes the topping when the tart is inverted onto a serving plate. The tart was created by two French sisters who lived in the Loire Valley and earned a living by making them.

1 package frozen puff pastry
2 tablespoons unsalted butter, softened
¼ cup sugar
2 Granny Smith apples, peeled, cored and cut into
  quarters
¼ cup fresh cranberries, optional

To prepare the puff pastry:
Preheat oven to 400 degrees.

Defrost the puff pastry according to directions on the package. Remove 1 sheet of puff pastry from the package. Place the sheet on a clean cutting board. Cut an 8-inch circle out of the sheet of pastry, using an 8-inch dish as a guide. Discard any puff pastry trimmings (unless you have another use for them).

To prepare the tart:
Spread the softened butter onto the bottom of an 8-inch oven proof, non-stick sauté pan. Sprinkle the sugar over the softened butter. Place the apple quarters in the pan on top of the butter and sugar mixture. If desired, cranberries may also be added to the pan, in and around the apple quarters. Place the pan over medium heat and cook until the sugar begins to caramelize.

When the sugar has caramelized, remove the pan from the heat. Lay the puff pastry circle over the top of the apples, tucking the pastry inside the pan around the outside of the apples.

Place the pan on the center rack of the preheated oven and bake for approximately 15 to 20 min-

utes, or until the puff pastry is completely baked. After removing the pan from the oven, invert it immediately onto a serving platter.

✧ **CHEF'S NOTE:** Serve immediately while still hot. This is delicious when served with vanilla ice cream or crème anglaise (the French word for English cream or custard cream).

ONE 8-INCH TART

⊹ VANILLA CRÈME BRULÉE

Professional chefs often use a small blowtorch, available in gourmet shops, to melt the sugar sprinkled on top of a crème brulée. If you don't happen to have a blowtorch handy, you can accomplish the same effect by placing the crème brulée under an oven broiler.

1 cup half-and-half
1 vanilla bean, cut in half lengthwise
$^1/_2$ teaspoon pure vanilla extract
1 egg
8 egg yolks
2/3 cup granulated sugar
1 and $^1/_2$ cups heavy cream, cold
4 tablespoons granulated sugar

Preparing the crème brulée:
Preheat oven to 325 degrees.

In a small saucepan, combine the half-and-half, vanilla bean and vanilla extract. Heat over medium-high heat just until scalded. Do not boil. Remove the vanilla bean.

Fill a large mixing bowl with ice and a little water. Set aside.

In a medium-size mixing bowl, stir the egg, egg yolks and 2/3 cup granulated sugar until combined. Gradually stir in the scalded mixture. Place the bowl in a larger bowl of ice water until mixture is completely cooled. Stir in heavy cream. Strain the mixture into a clean mixing bowl through a fine sieve or cheesecloth.

Divide the mixture evenly into 8 (4-ounce) ramekins. Place the filled ramekins in a baking dish just large enough to hold them. Add enough boiling water to the baking dish to come halfway up the sides of the ramekins. Bake in a 325-degree oven until the custard is set but still quivers in the center, approximately 35 minutes. Remove the ramekins from the baking dish and allow to cool. Cover each ramekin with plastic wrap. Refrigerate until completely chilled, at least 4 hours or overnight.

To caramelize the tops of the custards:
Sprinkle tablespoon of sugar on top of each custard. Using a broiler or small blowtorch, heat the top of the custard until the sugar is melted and caramelized, about 30 seconds. Watch carefully as sugar can burn easily. Serve while the sugar is still warm.

8 SERVINGS

→ CHOCOLATE PEAR TART

Almonds, chocolate and the delicate sweetness of pears, all in a rich butter crust, combine to make this most elegant dessert.

Poaching Liquid:

2 cups white wine

2 cups water

1 cup granulated sugar

1 cinnamon stick

1 or 2 cloves

5 fresh pears, peeled, sliced in half and cored

Chocolate Short Dough:

1 cup flour

$^1/_3$ cup sugar

$^1/_2$ cup cocoa powder

Pinch of salt

1 small egg

$^3/_4$ cup cold butter (1 and $^1/_4$ sticks)

Chocolate Frangipane:

1 and cups almond paste (available in specialty stores)

4 eggs

1 cup butter, at room temperature (2 sticks)

$^1/_3$ cup cake flour, sifted

$^1/_2$ cup cocoa powder

Apricot jam, for glazing

To poach the pears:

In a saucepan, combine all the poaching liquid ingredients over medium-high heat; bring to a simmer and poach the fruits for 10 to 15 minutes. The pears should be slightly firm when pierced with the tip of a sharp knife or a toothpick. Cover and refrigerate the pears in the poaching liquid.

To make the chocolate short dough:

In a food processor, combine all the dry ingredients using the dough knife. Pulse ingredients for 3 seconds. Add the egg and cold butter; mix for 15 seconds. Remove the dough from the processor and with your hands form a ball. Place the ball of dough on a lightly floured pan and refrigerate.

Roll out the dough with a rolling pin on a lightly floured surface until the dough has a diameter of approximately 14 inches. Grease an 11-inch tart pan and place the short dough inside. Set aside.

To make the chocolate frangipane:

Place the almond paste in a food processor and mix until smooth, about 5 seconds. Add 1 egg and incorporate. Add the softened butter and blend slowly together. Add the rest of the eggs, one at a time. Incorporate slowly.

Place the frangipane in a bowl. With a dough scraper, fold sifted flour and cocoa powder into the batter until well dispersed. Place the frangipane in a pastry bag, and pipe in a circular motion on the short dough covered tart form.

Using a sharp knife, cut the poached pears so they fan out evenly. Place the pears on top of the frangipane paste, starting in the middle and working outward.

To bake the tart:

Preheat oven to 375 degrees.

Place the tart on a sheet pan, and bake on the middle rack of the oven for 30 to 40 minutes, or until done. Use a knife to insert into the frangipane paste and check for doneness. Melt the apricot jam down into a liquid and glaze the top of the tart.

CHEF'S NOTE: The pears can be poached two days in advance and refrigerated in the poaching liquid. This will intensify the flavor of the pears.

ONE 11-INCH TART

GERMANY

✦ BEEF ROULADES

This traditional German dish consists of sliced beef rolled around a bacon, onion and pickle filling. The beef is braised and often served with spaetzle and braised red cabbage. A great Oktoberfest meal to enjoy with a hearty German beer.

12 (8-ounce) slices top round
Salt, freshly ground black pepper and paprika, to taste
Mustard, as needed
Ketchup, as needed
1 cup pickles, cut into thin julienne strips
1 pound bacon, cooked and chopped
1 large onion, diced and cooked with the bacon
1/2 cup butter, melted
2 tablespoons oil
1/3 cup chopped onions
1/3 cup chopped carrots
1/3 cup chopped celery
1 teaspoon tomato paste
2 tablespoons flour
1/4 cup dry red wine
6 cups beef broth
2 cups heavy cream, optional

To prepare the roulades:
Preheat oven to 400 degrees.

On a clean flat work surface, lay out the meat slices. With a meat mallet, flatten the slices until about 1/4-inch thick. Season the meat slices with salt, pepper and paprika. Smear the slices with mustard and ketchup. Place an equal amount of the pickles, bacon and onions on each of the meat slices. Roll the slices up to form roulades. Tie with kitchen string or secure with large toothpicks. Place the roulades in a roasting pan. Coat the roulades with melted butter.

Oven sear the roulades for 30 minutes or until evenly browned.

To make the braising sauce:
While the roulades are in the oven, heat the oil in a large frying pan. Add the onion, carrots and celery. Sauté until tender, about 15 minutes. Add the tomato paste. Cook for 1 minute. Add the flour. Stir until well blended. Add the wine, stirring well and scraping up the browned bits from the bottom of the frying pan. Add the broth and bring to a boil. Pour the braising sauce into the roasting pan containing the roulades. Cover the roasting pan and return it to the 400-degree oven. Braise for about 2 hours, turning the roulades occasionally.

Remove the pan from the oven. Transfer the roulades to a warm serving platter. Remove the kitchen string or toothpick from each roulade. Cover and keep warm.

Strain the sauce into a saucepan. Bring to a boil over high heat. Reduce the heat to low. Simmer until the sauce thickens. Season to taste with salt and pepper. If desired, heavy cream may be added to this sauce during the last 5 minutes of simmering.

To serve the roulades:
Pour the sauce over the roulades and serve immediately.

12 SERVINGS

→ SPAETZLE

Spaetzle are tiny flour dumplings originally from Germany. This versatile dish is best served with a hearty sauce. Other ingredients such as grated cheese, cooked bacon and chopped mushrooms may also be added for creativity and exciting flavor combinations.

2 to 2 and $^1/_2$ cups all-purpose flour
5 eggs
1 cup milk
Salt and freshly ground black pepper, to taste
4 ounces butter (1 stick)

To make spaetzle:
Fill a medium-size pot with lightly salted water and bring to a boil.

Combine all ingredients, except butter, and knead to a smooth dough. (Start with 2 cups of flour and add more if needed.) This is best when done by hand rather than machine.

Fill a spaetzle machine with the dough. Grate dough into the boiling water. Repeat until all dough is used. Simmer for 5 to 8 minutes. Drain spaetzle in a colander. Pour cooked spaetzle into a large skillet and sauté in butter.

✴ **CHEF'S NOTE:** A spaetzle machine can be purchased in large gourmet shops or through mail-order catalogs. Many home cooks improvise with metal colanders that have been coated with vegetable spray.

10 SERVINGS

→ BLACK FOREST CAKE

This famous cake comes from Germany's Black Forest region. It consists of layers of chocolate cake with cherries and chantilly, a sweetened cream sauce. Even more of this whipped cream is used to ice the entire cake which is then garnished with chocolate shavings and additional cherries.

Chocolate Sponge:

17 eggs

1 and 1/4 cups vegetable oil

1 and 1/4 cups milk

1 tablespoon vanilla extract

3 cups granulated sugar

3 and 1/4 cups cake flour

1/3 cup cocoa powder

2 tablespoons baking powder

1 teaspoon salt

2 and 1/4 teaspoons baking soda

Simple Syrup:

1/2 cup granulated sugar

1/2 cup water

1 lemon, sliced

Flavored Simple Syrup:

2 and 1/2 tablespoons simple syrup

2 tablespoons cherry syrup

1 tablespoon Kirschwasser (black cherry brandy)

Chantilly Cream:

1 quart heavy cream, well chilled

1/4 cup confectioner's sugar

2 teaspoons vanilla extract

Garnish:

3/4 cup canned dark cherries, drained

1/4 cup chocolate shavings

12 red maraschino cherries

To make the cake layers:

Preheat oven to 350 degrees.

Spray 4 (8-inch) cake pans thoroughly with non-stick cooking spray, and dust with flour.

In a mixing bowl, combine all the liquid ingredients. In a separate bowl, sift together all the dry ingredients. Place all the sifted dry ingredients on top of the liquid ingredients in bowl. Using an electric mixer, whip on low speed until all of the ingredients are blended slightly, approximately 30 seconds.

Whip for 4 minutes on high speed, scraping the bowl well. Whip for 3 minutes on medium speed, scraping the bowl well.

Divide the batter into the cake pans. Bake on the middle rack of the oven until the cakes are golden brown, 20 to 25 minutes. Cool for 5 to 10 minutes before removing cakes from pans. Slice each cake layer into 2 layers, each one about 1/2-inch thick.

To make the simple syrup:

In a small saucepan, combine the sugar and water over high heat and bring to a boil. Remove from heat and add the lemon slices. Cool. Store in refrigerator. Remove lemons before using.

To make the flavored simple syrup:

Blend all ingredients together and set aside.

To make the chantilly cream:

Place 2 cups of the heavy cream in a cold bowl and whip at high speed until cream thickens. Gradually add the remaining heavy cream. Mix until soft peaks form. Add the sugar and vanilla extract, and mix at medium speed until stiff peaks form. Use immediately or refrigerate until needed.

To assemble the cake:

Moisten each cake layer with the flavored simple syrup. Make certain the cake layers are completely cool before assembling.

Pipe a target pattern in Chantilly cream on the first cake layer. To do this, pipe a dot in the center, a $1/2$-inch bead around the outside edge, and finally a $1/2$-inch circle between the dot and the perimeter. Between these lines of Chantilly cream, spoon the dark cherries until the space is completely filled. You should have alternating circles of Chantilly cream and cherries.

Place the second layer of sponge on top of the Chantilly cream and cherries. Repeat the same for the second layer; only one circle of cherries is needed for this layer. Continue to do this with every layer of sponge cake topped with the Chantilly cream and cherries, and pressing down firmly with each new cake layer.

Use the Chantilly cream to ice the entire cake, starting at the top and working your way down the sides, using a knife or cake spatula.

Place the chocolate shavings on the sides of the cake. Divide and mark 12 portions evenly by piping Chantilly cream rosettes with a star tube 1/4-inch from the edge of the torte. Garnish the center of the torte with chocolate shavings. Place a maraschino cherry on each rosette.

✳ **CHEF'S NOTE:** You may use sweet or tart dark cherries. If they are large, cut them in half. If desired, these cherries may be soaked overnight in 2 tablespoons of Kirschwasser. To make the chocolate shavings, use a box grater or vegetable peeler.

ONE 8-INCH CAKE

SCANDINAVIA

↝ BREAKFAST WAFFLES WITH BLACKBERRY SYRUP

The honeycombed surface of waffles is perfect for holding pockets of syrup. In this version, fresh blackberries are turned into a warm fruit topping for the crisp, light waffles.

3 large eggs
1 cup milk
1 tablespoon vanilla extract
1/2 cup butter, melted (1 stick)
2 cups flour
1 tablespoon baking powder
2 teaspoons sugar
1/2 teaspoon salt

To make the waffle batter:
Preheat waffle iron.

In a medium-size mixing bowl, combine the eggs with the milk, vanilla extract and melted butter. Beat thoroughly.

In a separate bowl, combine all the dry ingredients. Slowly add the dry ingredients to the egg mixture. Beat until well mixed. Allow batter to rest for 10 minutes before using.

Following the manufacturer's directions for your waffle iron, pour the batter (usually a rounded cup per waffle) onto the preheated waffle iron. Cook for 2 to 3 minutes or to desired doneness. Serve with warm Blackberry Syrup (recipe follows).

4 SERVINGS

Blackberry Syrup
1 pint fresh blackberries
1/2 cup maple syrup

In a blender on high speed, combine the blackberries and maple syrup. Purée until smooth. Pour the mixture into a small saucepan and heat the syrup.

✷ **CHEF'S NOTE:** This syrup is a bit on the tart side. If desired, additional maple syrup can be used to sweeten it.

MAKES ABOUT 2 CUPS

→ HONEY CILANTRO CURED GRAVLAX

Gravlax is a delicate, cured salmon appetizer which should be made with the freshest salmon available. The sugar and salt combination cures and firms the fillets. Serve gravlax with wedges of fresh lemon, capers and French bread or light rye and sweet butter.

3 bunches fresh dill, chopped

3 bunches fresh cilantro, chopped

$2/3$ cup sugar

$2/3$ cup kosher salt

$1/2$ cup coarsely ground black pepper

$1/2$ cup coriander seeds, toasted

2 tablespoons honey

1 (6-pound) salmon, filleted (skin on)

To make the gravlax rub:

Combine the first 4 ingredients. Place the pepper and coriander seeds in a coffee grinder. Mill until fine. Add to other ingredients along with the honey. Mix thoroughly.

To cure the salmon:

Make sure that there are no bones in the salmon fillets. If you find bones, remove them with tweezers or long-nosed pliers.

Place a large sheet of aluminum foil in a 4-inch deep roasting pan. Place a layer of plastic wrap on top of the foil. Place 1 salmon fillet on the plastic wrap, skin side down. Add half the cure mixture onto the salmon. Rub lightly into the flesh of the salmon. Repeat this process with the other salmon side. Place the salmon sides together with flesh side touching flesh side.

Wrap tightly with plastic wrap, then wrap with aluminum foil. Center the wrapped salmon in the roasting pan.

On top, place another roasting pan which is filled with large canned goods to use as weights. Refrigerate. Turn the salmon once a day. Allow to cure for 3 to 4 days.

To serve the Gravlax:

Remove the salmon from the refrigerator and unwrap. Scrape off all the cure ingredients. Slice the salmon paper thin, starting from the tail end. Slice on the bias working towards the tail. Leftover gravlax should be wrapped tightly in plastic wrap and refrigerated. It also may be frozen.

✳ **CHEF'S NOTE:** If you do not have a coffee grinder, use ground pepper and ground coriander seeds, available in the spice section of supermarkets. If using ground spices, reduce the amounts to 1/4 cup each. Chopping the dill and cilantro may be done by hand or in a food processor.

24 SERVINGS

↙ POACHED VEAL SHANKS WITH DILL SAUCE

This simple recipe yields tender veal and vegetables - great for a cozy winter supper. Poaching is a cooking method in which items are cooked gently in simmering liquid.

1 onion, chopped

2, 2-inch pieces of leek, cut into halves

1 carrot, cut into 1-inch pieces

4 veal shanks

Enough cold water to cover the veal shanks during poaching

3 tablespoons white wine vinegar

Dill stems

1 bay leaf

10 whole black peppercorns

Sauce:

1 tablespoon butter

1 tablespoon flour

2 cups veal stock (from poaching the shanks)

3 tablespoons heavy cream

Salt, freshly ground black pepper and sugar, to taste

1 tablespoon white wine vinegar

1/2 cup finely chopped dill

To poach the veal shanks:

In a deep pan, place the onions, leeks and carrots. Place the veal shanks on top of the vegetables. Add enough cold water to cover the shanks. Add the vinegar and spices. Slowly bring to a boil. Lower the heat to a simmer to poach the meat. Add more water if too much evaporates. Poach for 45 minutes to 1 hour, until the meat is tender. Skim the surface of the water, if necessary.

To make the sauce:

In a saucepan over medium-high heat, melt the butter. Add the flour to make a roux. Slowly add the veal stock, making sure there are no lumps. Add the cream. Season to taste with the salt, pepper, sugar and vinegar. Blend well. Strain the sauce. Just before serving, add the finely chopped dill. Serve with boiled root vegetables and potatoes.

4 SERVINGS

✣ BRAISED BEEF SHORT RIBS

Braising is a cooking method in which the main item, usually meat, is seared in fat, then simmered in stock or another liquid in a covered vessel. The results are meat that is tender and falling off the bone.

4 beef short ribs

Salt and freshly ground black pepper, to taste

1 cup all-purpose flour, seasoned with salt and pepper

2 tablespoons oil

2 cups beef broth

2 carrots, peeled and cut into 1-inch pieces

2 parsnips, peeled and cut into 1-inch pieces

1 Spanish onion, peeled and cut into 1-inch pieces

1 bay leaf

1 tablespoon juniper berries

1 teaspoon whole black peppercorns

To sear the beef and vegetables:

Season the beef short ribs with salt and pepper. Dust the ribs with seasoned flour. In a skillet over high heat, heat the oil and sear the ribs until golden brown on all sides. Move the ribs into a deep braising pan.

In the same skillet, sear the vegetables until golden brown on all sides. Pour the vegetables over the ribs in the deep braising pan. Deglaze the skillet with the beef broth and pour the broth over the ribs and vegetables.

To braise the beef and vegetables:

Preheat oven to 325 degrees.

Add the spices to the ribs and vegetables. Cover and braise in the oven for 1 to 2 hours or until the meat is tender.

4 SERVINGS

AMERICA

⊹ ROASTED CORN AND LOBSTER JOHNNY CAKES

Considered to be the precursor to the pancake, the johnnycake dates back to the early 1700s. It is a flat griddlecake made of cornmeal, salt and either boiling water or milk. These roasted corn johnnycakes are topped with fresh lobster meat and finished with a sherried crème fraîche.

3 cups johnnycake meal

2 and 2/3 cups milk

3 eggs

1 cup roasted corn kernels (recipe follows)

1 teaspoon salt

1 teaspoon baking powder

1 and pounds cooked lobster meat, cut into bite-size pieces

1 tablespoon butter

Garnish:

Sherried crème frâiche, as needed

Basil oil, as needed

Fresh chives, as needed

To make the johnnycakes:

Combine the johnnycake meal, milk, eggs, roasted corn kernels, salt and baking powder. Mix well. Spoon a heaping tablespoon of the mixture onto a hot, lightly oiled, non-stick cooking pan. As the johnnycakes brown, turn them over. Cook until golden brown on both sides. Keep warm.

If desired, an electric frying pan set at 325 degrees may be used.

Pick over the cooked lobster meat, making sure all bits of shell have been removed. Sauté the lobster meat in the butter. Set aside.

To serve the johnnycakes:

Place 3 warm johnnycakes on each plate. Top with the sautéed lobster meat. Drizzle with sherried crème fraîche (recipe follows). Decorate each plate with drops of basil oil (recipe follows). Garnish with fresh chives.

Roasted Corn Kernels

4 ears fresh corn on the cob

¹/₄ cup melted butter

Salt and freshly ground black pepper, to taste

To roast the corn:

Preheat oven to 425 degrees.

Husk the corn, and place the ears on a baking sheet. Brush the corn with the melted butter. Season with salt and pepper. Place the pan in the oven, turning the ears every 10 minutes until golden.

Remove the corn from the oven, and allow to cool. With a sharp knife, strip the kernels off each cob. Set the roasted corn kernels aside for the johnnycake recipe.

Sherried Crème Frâiche

1 tablespoon butter

¹/₄ cup shallots, chopped fine

¹/₄ cup dry sherry

1 cup heavy cream

1 cup sour cream

Salt and white pepper, to taste

In a saucepan over medium-high heat, melt the butter. Add the shallots. Remove the saucepan from the heat. Add the sherry, reduce by half. Allow to cool. Add the heavy cream and sour cream. Season to taste with salt and white pepper. Place in a squirt bottle and refrigerate.

Basil Oil

¹/₂ cup olive oil

1 bunch fresh basil, stemmed

To make the basil oil:

In a saucepan, heat the olive oil over medium heat for 2 minutes. Remove from the heat. Add the fresh basil, stir and allow to cool. Place the mixture in a food processor and puree until smooth. Place in a squirt bottle and set aside for garnishing each plate. Refrigerate any leftover basil oil.

6 SERVINGS

⇢ LINGUINE FRITTATA AND TRI-COLORED HOME-FRIED POTATOES

This open-faced pasta omelet is topped with oven-roasted plum tomatoes and tender sweet Italian sausage, then finished with shaved Pecorino-Romano cheese. Served with these unusual and colorful home-fries, it makes a great dish for a festive Sunday Brunch.

Linguine Frittata

1 pound ground sweet Italian sausage

4 large eggs, beaten

1/2 cup shredded mozzarella cheese

1/8 cup basil, cut into fine strips

1/2 pound linguine, cooked al dente

Oven-dried Roma tomatoes (prepared the night before, recipe follows)

2 ounces Pecorino-Romano cheese, shaved to order

Italian flat leaf parsley, as needed, for garnish

To prepare the frittata:

Preheat the oven to 350 degrees.

In a large oven-proof sauté pan over medium-high heat, cook the ground sausage until completely browned. Drain excess fat. Set pan aside.

In a large mixing bowl, combine the beaten eggs, mozzarella cheese and basil. Add this mixture to the drained sausage meat in the sauté pan. Over medium heat, cook this mixture until it becomes firm on the bottom. Use a spatula to check the bottom which should be solid while the top is still liquid. Add the linguine to the egg mixture. Top with the oven-dried tomatoes.

Place the pan in the preheated oven and bake until the top sets and turns golden brown, approximately 25 to 30 minutes, or until a knife inserted into the frittata comes out clean. Remove the sauté pan from the oven, cover and allow to set for 10 minutes. Just before serving, top with shaved Pecorino-Romano cheese. Cut the omelet into wedges, garnish with Italian flat leaf parsley, and serve immediately with Tri-Colored Home-Fried Potatoes (recipe follows).

Oven-Dried Roma Tomatoes

6 Roma tomatoes

Salt and freshly ground black pepper, to taste

To oven-dry the tomatoes:

Preheat the oven to 350 degrees.

Wash the tomatoes. Cut in half lengthwise from core to tip. Place the tomatoes cut side down on a baking sheet. Season the tomatoes with salt and black pepper. Place the sheet pan of tomatoes in the oven, bake for 15 minutes, and then shut off the oven. Remove the tomatoes from the oven the following day.

6-8 SERVINGS

Tri-Colored Home-Fried Potatoes

¹/₄ cup clarified butter

¹/₄ cup olive oil

1 cup sliced Vidalia (or other sweet) onions

2 garlic cloves, minced

1 pound Yukon gold potatoes, diced

1 pound sweet potatoes, diced

1 pound purple potatoes, diced

Salt and freshly ground black pepper, to taste

1 teaspoon fresh or dried thyme

To prepare the potatoes:

In a very large sauté pan over medium-high heat, combine the clarified butter and olive oil (do not brown). Add the sliced onions to the hot pan. Sauté until translucent. Lower the heat and add the garlic. Add all the diced potatoes, mixing them well with the onions. Brown evenly, and cook until the potatoes are tender, approximately 20 minutes. Season to taste with salt, pepper and fresh thyme.

CHEF'S NOTE: Clarified butter, also known as drawn butter, is unsalted butter that has been slowly melted to separate the milk solids (which sink to the bottom of the pan) from the golden liquid on the surface. After any foam is skimmed off the top, the clear butter is poured off the milky residue for use in cooking. Because the milk solids have been removed, clarified butter has a higher smoke point than regular butter and may be used to cook at higher temperatures. On the down side, this also means that the clarified butter will not have as rich a flavor.

6-8 SERVINGS

→ GRILLED PORK LOIN WITH APPLE BARBECUE SAUCE

This grilled pork loin is very easy to make and comes out moist and flavorful. The unusual combination of flavors in the barbecue sauce puts a new twist on a traditional recipe.

1 medium-size boneless pork loin, partially trimmed (2 to 3 pounds)
¼ cup vegetable oil
Salt and freshly ground black pepper, to taste

To grill the pork loin:

Rub the whole pork loin with oil. Season with salt and pepper. Heat grill to high temperature and then turn to low. Place the meat on the grill and sear evenly on all sides. Place the meat on the inside shelf (if the grill has this feature) to cook indirectly. If there is no inside shelf, turn the meat frequently to prevent it from burning. Close the lid and grill until the meat reaches an internal temperature of 165 to 175 degrees on a meat thermometer. Brush on some of the Apple Barbecue Sauce (recipe follows) and serve immediately.

Apple Barbecue Sauce
½ cup butter (1 stick)
1 large yellow onion, diced fine
¼ cup brown sugar
1 garlic clove, minced
1 cup ketchup
3 tablespoons Worcestershire sauce
½ cup beef stock
¼ cup red wine vinegar
1 can cola beverage
½ cup applesauce
1 apple, peeled and diced, for garnish

To make the sauce:

In a large skillet, melt the butter. Sauté the onions in the butter until translucent. Add the sugar. Cook for 5 minutes over medium heat, stirring occasionally. Add remaining ingredients, except the diced apple, and bring to a boil. Reduce the heat and simmer for 15 minutes. Serve the sauce with grilled pork loin, garnished with diced apple.

6 SERVINGS

→ CAJUN-YANKEE GUMBO

Gumbo is a thick soup traditionally made with okra, tomatoes, vegetables and chicken, shrimp, oysters, crab and/or ham. This Yankee version puts a Northern spin on this very Southern dish. File powder is made from sassafras leaves and is widely used in Creole cooking.

Roux:
1 cup vegetable oil
1 and $^1/_2$ cups flour

Base:
3 quarts seafood stock (or canned clam juice)
2 cups chopped onions
1 cup chopped celery
1 cup chopped bell peppers (red, green and yellow)
$^1/_4$ cup minced garlic
$^1/_2$ cup thinly sliced scallions, white part only
1 (28-ounce) can crushed tomatoes in juice
Salt, freshly ground black pepper and Tabasco sauce, to taste
1 (10-ounce) package frozen okra, thawed

Seasoning:
2 teaspoons garlic powder
2 teaspoons onion powder
1 teaspoon thyme
1 teaspoon Spanish paprika
1 teaspoon chervil
1 teaspoon freshly ground black pepper
$^1/_2$ teaspoon basil
$^1/_2$ teaspoon oregano

Main Ingredients:
Vegetable oil, as needed
1 pound andouille sausage (or chorizo)
32 shrimp (26 to 30 per pound), peeled and deveined
4 small lobster tails, split
1 pound lump crab meat
2 dozen oysters, shucked
File powder, as needed (optional)

Accompaniments:
8 cups cooked white rice
2 tablespoons chopped scallion greens
2 tablespoons chopped parsley

To make the roux:
In a medium-size saucepan over medium-high heat, combine the oil and flour, stirring constantly, until the mixture begins to turn dark brown.

To make the base:
In a large stock pot, heat the seafood stock to a simmer. To the stock, add the chopped onions, celery, bell peppers, garlic, scallions and tomatoes. Cook over medium-high heat until the vegetables become soft. Strain the stock, discarding the vegetables. Slowly combine the strained stock and the roux, blending well to avoid lumps. Season with salt, pepper and Tabasco sauce. Add the okra. Allow base to simmer for 30 minutes.

To season the main ingredients:

Combine the seasoning ingredients. Oil and season the andouille sausage, shrimp and lobster tails. Set aside.

To prepare the sausage and seafood:

Preheat the grill. Place the sausage, shrimp and lobster tails on the grill, being careful not to burn the meat and seafood. Once the sausage is cooked, cut into 1-inch chunks and add to simmering stock pot. Add the cooked shrimp, lobster, crab meat and oysters. Stir well. Season to taste. Bring back to a boil. The gumbo is now ready to serve. Just before serving, sprinkle with a little file powder, if desired.

To serve the gumbo:

Place a generous mound of cooked white rice in the center of a large bowl. Ladle the gumbo around the rice, making sure each dish has a lobster tail. Garnish with chopped scallion greens and chopped parsley.

✳ **CHEF'S NOTE:** The main ingredients for gumbo can include sausage and seafood as in this recipe, but the seafood can be replaced with chicken for a less expensive dish. Leftover gumbo may be frozen and reheated at a later time.

12 SERVINGS

→ RHODE ISLAND SEAFOOD STRUDEL

In this dish, tender scallops, shrimp and crab are baked in phyllo dough until golden brown and crispy, then served with a dill cream reduction. The strudel is a great luncheon entree when served with a crisp green salad.

Poaching Liquid:
$1/4$ cup chopped onion
$1/4$ cup chopped celery
$1/4$ cup chopped leeks, white part only
1 teaspoon peppercorns
2 bay leaves
4 parsley stems
4 cups cold water
1 cup white wine

Seafood:
$1/2$ pound scallops, cleaned and patted dry
$1/2$ pound shrimp, peeled and deveined
$1/2$ pound crab meat, picked over and drained

Seafood Dill Cream Reduction:
$1/2$ cup heavy cream
1 cup seafood poaching liquid
1 tablespoon chopped dill

Strudel:
$1/2$ cup melted butter
1 package frozen phyllo dough sheets*
Old Bay seafood seasoning, to taste

Egg Wash:
1 egg
1 tablespoon milk

Garnish:
Fresh dill sprigs, as needed
6 whole poached shrimp

*Thaw the package of frozen phyllo dough sheets in the refrigerator a day in advance. Allow the package of phyllo dough sheets to sit at room temperature for 20 minutes before starting this recipe.

To prepare the poaching liquid:
In a large saucepan over medium-high heat, combine all the poaching liquid ingredients, and simmer for no more than 45 minutes. Strain, discard the vegetable mixture, and set the poaching liquid aside.

To prepare the seafood:
Place the scallops and shrimp in the strained poaching liquid. Cook very quickly, 2 to 3 minutes, over medium-high heat until the shrimp turn pink. Drain, reserving the liquid. Allow the scallops and shrimp to cool. Save 6 poached shrimp to garnish the serving plates. Cut the remaining shrimp into pieces. Mix the scallops and shrimp with the crab meat. Refrigerate.

To make the seafood dill cream reduction:

In a saucepan, heat the heavy cream and reduce by half. Add 1 cup poaching liquid. Reduce until slightly thickened. Add the chopped dill.

To make the strudel:

Preheat the oven to 400 degrees.

Mix a small amount of the seafood dill cream reduction into the seafood.

Remove the phyllo dough from the package, place on a clean work surface, and cover with a damp towel. Peel off the first sheet of dough, and place on a non-stick baking sheet pan. Brush with the melted butter. Sprinkle with the seafood seasoning. Repeat this process 4 more times, placing the sheets on top of one another. Brush the last sheet with melted butter and top with the seafood mixture. Roll the layers of dough into a cylinder. Tuck in the edges.

Combine the eggs and milk to make an egg wash. Brush the strudel with the egg wash.

With a very sharp knife, score the top of the strudel, dividing it into 6 equal portions (these slashes in the dough will also act as air vents). Bake until golden brown, approximately 20 minutes.

Remove the strudel from the oven and cut into 6 portions, using the score marks as a guide. Place some of the sauce on each serving plate, and place the strudel on the sauce. Garnish each serving with a fresh dill sprig and a poached shrimp.

6 SERVINGS

→ DUCK BREAST SANDWICH WITH GORGONZOLA CHEESE AND SLICED APPLES

Tired of the same old sandwiches? Surprise your family and friends with this tasty duck breast sandwich. The unusual mix of flavors will tickle their taste buds and have them coming back for more.

1 boneless, skinless duck breast, about 12 ounces

1 tablespoon brown sugar

1 tablespoon salt

2 flax seed (or other whole grain) rolls,* sliced open

1 tablespoon whole grain mustard

1 tablespoon honey

¹/₂ cup fresh basil leaves, washed

1 Granny Smith apple, peeled, cored and sliced thin

4 ounces Gorgonzola cheese

*a recipe for Multi purpose flax seed bread can be found on page 121 of this book.

To prepare the duck breast:

In a bowl, combine the duck breast with the sugar and salt. Mix well. Cover and refrigerate overnight. The next day, rinse the duck and pat dry.

Prepare the grill. Grill the duck breast over medium heat until medium rare, approximately 4 minutes on each side or until it reaches a temperature of 135 degrees on an instant-read meat thermometer. Set the duck breast aside. Grill the flax seed rolls until crisp, 1 to 2 minutes. Set the rolls aside.

To make the sandwiches:

In another bowl, combine the mustard and honey. On the bottom half of each roll, spread the mustard and honey mixture. Cut the duck breast into thin slices. Place the slices of duck breast on each roll, then top with basil leaves, apple slices and Gorgonzola cheese. Cover the sandwich with the top half of the roll. Serve at once.

2 SERVINGS

→ SMOKED TURKEY SANDWICH WITH ROASTED GARLIC SALSA

The fresh herb salsa turns an ordinary turkey sandwich into a very special lunch offering. Not your typical day-after-Thanksgiving fare!

2 beefsteak tomatoes, diced

1/2 English cucumber, diced

1/2 cup chopped fresh basil

2 tablespoons chopped scallions

1 tablespoon chopped Italian parsley

1 teaspoon chopped fresh thyme

1 tablespoon chopped roasted garlic

2 tablespoons olive oil

1 tablespoon wine vinegar

Salt and freshly ground black pepper, to taste

4 flax seed (or other whole grain) rolls,* sliced open

1 head radicchio lettuce, washed and drained

1 pound smoked turkey breast, sliced 1/8-inch thick

* A recipe for multi purpose flax seed bread can be found on page 121 of this book.

To make the fresh herb salsa:

In a large bowl, combine the tomatoes, cucumbers, basil, scallions, parsley, thyme, roasted garlic, oil and vinegar. Gently toss. Season to taste with salt and pepper.

To make the sandwiches:

Lightly grill the rolls or heat them in an oven. On the bottom half of each roll, place a leaf of radicchio, then 1/4 pound of smoked turkey. Top with the fresh herb salsa. Cover the sandwich with the top half of the roll. Slice in half. Serve at once.

✳ **CHEF'S NOTE:** To make roasted garlic, slice about 1/4 of an inch off the top of an entire garlic bulb. Drizzle the bulb with olive oil. Season to taste with salt and freshly ground black pepper. Wrap the bulb in aluminum foil and place in a preheated 350-degree oven for 20 minutes. Remove from the oven and unwrap. Gently squeeze the roasted garlic from each clove within the bulb into a bowl. Roasted garlic is also delicious when used as a spread on French or Italian bread.

4 SERVINGS

→ GRILLED VEGETABLE SANDWICH WITH GORGONZOLA DRESSING

This is a most delicious way to get your daily allotment of vegetables. Everything from the garden is in this sandwich, from arugula to zucchini.

Marinade:

$^1/_2$ cup olive oil

3 tablespoons white balsamic vinegar

1 tablespoon finely chopped fresh basil

1 teaspoon finely chopped fresh rosemary

1 tablespoon finely chopped Italian parsley

$^1/_2$ teaspoon kosher salt

$^1/_8$ teaspoon freshly ground black pepper

1 large zucchini

1 large yellow squash

2 Japanese eggplant

1 large Vidalia (or other sweet) onion

4 portobello mushrooms

Dressing:

$^1/_2$ cup imported Gorgonzola cheese, chopped

$^2/_3$ cup mayonnaise

2 tablespoons fresh lemon juice

1 tablespoon chopped fresh basil

1 teaspoon chopped fresh tarragon

1 tablespoon chopped Italian parsley

1 tablespoon capers, rinsed and chopped

Freshly ground black pepper, to taste

1 loaf flax seed (or other whole grain) bread, sliced

1 bunch arugula, washed with stems removed

1 yellow beefsteak tomato, cut into $^1/_4$ -inch slices

1 red beefsteak tomato, cut into $^1/_4$ -inch slices

To prepare the marinade:

In a bowl, combine the oil, vinegar, basil, rosemary, parsley, salt and pepper.

To prepare the vegetables:

Cut the zucchini, yellow squash, eggplant and onion into 1/4-inch thick slices. Arrange the sliced vegetables and the mushrooms on a sheet pan. Lightly brush all the vegetables with the marinade.

To grill the vegetables:

Prepare the grill. Over medium heat, grill the sliced vegetables for 2 minutes on each side or until the vegetables have softened. Place the grilled vegetables on a platter. Set aside.

To make the dressing:

In a bowl, combine the Gorgonzola cheese and mayonnaise. Mix well. Add the lemon juice, fresh herbs, capers and pepper. Blend well.

To assemble each sandwich:

Spread 1 tablespoon of dressing on a slice of bread. Add a few leaves of arugula, then a variety of the grilled vegetables. Top with slices of yellow and red beefsteak tomatoes and another slice of bread. Carefully slice in half. Serve at once.

4 SERVINGS

✦ MULTI-PURPOSE FLAX SEED BREAD

Flax seeds have been around for ages but have only recently been discovered by health-conscious food lovers. What makes the seeds so nutritious is the abundance of lineolic acid and omega-3 oil. These elements make flax an ideal food for building the good kind of cholesterol (HDL) and fighting the bad kind (LDL). They are also an excellent source of fiber, vitamins and minerals.

1 tablespoon instant yeast or 1 and $^1/_4$ tablespoons
active dry yeast
1 cup buttermilk or low-fat milk, lukewarm
3 and $^1/_2$ cups high-gluten bread flour
1 cup ground flax seeds
1 and $^1/_2$ teaspoons sea salt or table salt
(or 2 and $^1/_2$ teaspoons kosher salt)
4 tablespoons honey or brown sugar
$^1/_2$ to $^3/_4$ cup water, at room temperature

*2 tablespoons whole flax seed, optional, for garnishing
the top of the loaves*

To make the flax seed bread:

If using active dry yeast, dissolve it in the lukewarm buttermilk for 5 minutes. Instant yeast can be added directly to the dough.

In a food processor using the metal, not plastic, blade, mix all of the ingredients except the water. Or you may mix the ingredients by hand in a mixing bowl. Add the water a little at a time until the ingredients form a firm but pliable ball of dough. If using a food processor, let the ball of dough rest for 5 minutes, then mix for 45 seconds. If mixing by hand, sprinkle some flour on the counter and transfer the dough to the counter and knead by hand for about 10 minutes, or until the dough is smooth, slightly tacky but not sticky, and supple. Add more flour or water if necessary while kneading to achieve this consistency. The dough should feel just slightly warm.

Lightly oil a 4-quart mixing bowl and place the dough in the bowl, rolling it to coat the entire piece of dough with oil. Cover the bowl with plastic wrap and let the dough rise for 90 minutes to 2 hours, or until doubled in size.

Divide the dough into the desired size pieces with a pastry blade or serrated bread knife. Sandwich loaf breads should be cut according to the size pan you will be using. A 1-pound loaf is usually baked in a pan that is 4 inches wide by 8 and $^1/_2$ inches long. A 2-pound loaf is baked in a pan that is usually 5 inches wide by 9 inches long. Free standing loaves and rolls should be baked on a sheet pan that has been covered with baking parchment. It does not need to be oiled. Shape the dough into the desired shapes and place in the appropriate pan or pans. If making rolls, space them about 2 inches apart. Mist the top of the dough with vegetable oil spray and loosely cover the dough with plastic wrap. Let the dough rise for approximately 90 minutes, or until nearly but not quite doubled in size. Sandwich loaf bread should be cresting about 1 inch above the pan.

While the dough is rising, preheat the oven to 350 degrees for loaf bread, 400 degrees for small dinner rolls, and 375 degrees for hoagie or torpedo rolls. Mist the top of the dough with water from a sprayer and sprinkle the whole flax seeds on the tops (optional). Bake the bread on the middle shelf of the oven, 15 to 20 minutes for rolls, approximately 35 minutes for picnic breads, and about 45 to 60 minutes for sandwich bread. The bread should be a deep golden brown all around and should sound hollow when thumped on the bottom. The internal temperature of the bread, in the center, should be between 185 to 195 degrees (you can use an instant-read thermometer if you have one).

Transfer the bread from the pans to a cooling rack and allow to cool for 20 minutes for rolls and 40 to 60 minutes for loaves, longer (90 minutes at least) if planning to slice immediately for sandwiches. Store the completely cooled bread in a sealed plastic bag.

CHEF'S NOTE: In the dough, the flax seed "flour" is 33 percent the weight of the bread flour, giving the bread loads of fiber and other health benefits. The flax has no gluten so in order to achieve a light loaf, it's best to use high-gluten bread flour rather than all-purpose flour or whole-wheat flour. However, for those who love dense whole-grain bread, feel free to replace the bread flour with whole-wheat flour. This dough is very versatile and can be used for sandwich loaves, dinner rolls, hoagie or torpedo rolls, and even for free-standing picnic loaves (boules, batards or baguettes). It is slightly sweet with a nutty flavor from the flax seeds.

(MAKES 2 POUNDS OF DOUGH, ENOUGH FOR
1 LARGE OR 2 SMALL SANDWICH LOAVES,
3 OR 4 FREE-STANDING LOAVES, OR 8 TO 16
ROLLS, DEPENDING ON THE SIZE)

✢ SPICY GRILLED CATFISH WITH MANGO AND CUCUMBER SALSA

This cooling fresh salsa takes the bite out of the fiery Cajun seasoning. More or less Cajun seasoning can be used, depending on how much cold beer is available.

Mango and Cucumber Salsa:

1 mango, peeled and chopped

¹/₂ cucumber, peeled, seeded and chopped

1 tablespoon red onion, diced small

1 tablespoon red bell pepper, diced small

1 jalapeno pepper, diced fine

1 tablespoon chopped cilantro

1 tablespoon lime juice

Salt, to taste

4 (6-ounce) catfish fillets

Canola oil, as needed

1 tablespoon Cajun seasoning

Making the salsa:

Combine all the salsa ingredients. Cover and refrigerate for about 1 hour to allow time for the flavors to mingle.

Preparing the catfish:

Brush the catfish fillets with canola oil. Rub each fillet with Cajun seasoning. Lay the catfish on a platter and refrigerate while the grill is preheating.

Grilling the catfish:

Preheat the grill to medium-high heat. Oil the grill well and place the fish presentation side down. Turn the fish over when it is about half done, approximately 4 minutes. Continue to cook the fish until it flakes with a fork, another 3 to 4 minutes.

4 SERVINGS

⇥ APPLE CRISP FRENCH TOAST

This not so traditional French toast is prepared with thick sliced French bread, layered with Cortland apples, browned on both sides, topped with streusel and served with real maple syrup, fresh whipped cream and a sprinkle of ground cinnamon.

Crisp Topping:

1 cup oatmeal
¹/₄ pound butter, softened (1 stick)
1 pinch cinnamon
¹/₄ cup brown sugar
¹/₄ cup flour

Batter:

4 cups milk
4 eggs
1 vanilla bean (or 1 teaspoon vanilla extract)
2 tablespoons sugar
Cinnamon, pinch

1 loaf French bread, cut into thick slices on an angle
3 Cortland apples, peeled, cored, sliced, held in water and lemon juice

Maple syrup, as needed
Whipped cream, as needed
Ground cinnamon, as needed

To make the crisp topping:

Preheat oven to 350 degrees.

Place the oatmeal on a baking sheet and bake for 5 minutes. In a large bowl, combine the toasted oatmeal with the softened butter, cinnamon, brown sugar and pastry flour. Mix well. Place the mixture on a baking sheet and bake until crisp but not hard, about 5 minutes. Allow to cool.

To make the batter:

Combine the milk and eggs, beating well. Split the vanilla bean open and scrape the contents into the milk and egg mixture. Add the sugar and cinnamon; mix well. Set aside.

To prepare the French toast:

Preheat oven to 350 degrees.

Dip the bread slices in the egg batter. Place the bread slices in a hot non-stick pan, and brown on both sides. Place the cooked French toast slices on a non-stick baking pan. Top the French toast with the sliced apples. Top the apples with the crisp topping.

Bake for 30 minutes or until the French toast is hot and the apples are just cooked. Place the French toast on a serving plate, drizzle with maple syrup, garnish with a little whipped cream, and sprinkle with ground cinnamon.

6 SERVINGS

⇥ SOUTHWESTERN STUFFED ZUCCHINI

This recipe can be modified in a number of different ways to match your entrée and ingredients you may have on hand. Yellow neck squash may be substituted for zucchini; Monterey jack cheese for queso fresco; oregano for cilantro, to name just a few variations.

4 small zucchini, about 1 pound
4 ounces queso fresco or Monterey Jack cheese, cut into strips
Olive oil, as needed
1 tablespoon cilantro, finely chopped
Freshly ground black pepper, to taste

Preparing the zucchini:
Cut a 1/4-inch lengthwise wedge out of each zucchini. Stuff the zucchini with strips of cheese. Sprinkle with olive oil, cilantro and black pepper. Loosely wrap the zucchini in aluminum foil.

Grilling the zucchini:
Preheat grill to medium high heat. Place the zucchini on the grill and cook until tender, approximately 20 minutes. When soft, carefully open the foil and transfer the zucchini to a serving platter.

⋆ **CHEF'S NOTE:** Be careful not to let the foil come into contact with the cheese because the cheese will burn and stick to the foil.

4 SERVINGS

→GRILLED NEW YORK STRIP STEAKS WITH BALSAMIC GLAZED BERMUDA ONIONS

There's nothing better on the grill than New York strip steaks accompanied by Bermuda onions that have been glazed with balsamic vinegar. A true beef lovers delight!

3-pound whole beef sirloin strip, trimmed and boneless
1 tablespoon garlic powder
2 tablespoons coarsely ground black pepper
Kosher salt, as needed
3 Bermuda onions, peeled
2 tablespoons olive oil
2 tablespoons balsamic vinegar
Salt and freshly ground black pepper, to taste

To prepare the steak:

Allow the steak to sit at room temperature for 15 minutes before grilling.

Preheat the grill to medium-high heat. If using charcoal or charwood, set the coals on one side of the grill to cook the meat with indirect heat.

Season the steak with garlic powder, coarsely ground black pepper and kosher salt.

To prepare the onions:

Cut the onions into sixths, slicing directly through the core each time, so that the onions are cut into wedges. Lay the cut onions in equal rows on a cutting board with the wide side of the onions all facing in the same direction. Carefully run a metal skewer through the middle of the onions. Lay the skewered onions on a cookie sheet, and drizzle with olive oil and balsamic vinegar. Season to taste with salt and pepper.

To grill the steak and the onions:

Place the meat fat side down on the hot side of the grill. Brown the meat on both sides, then move the meat to the cold side of the grill to cook with indirect heat. If using a gas grill, shut the gas off on the indirect side.

Place the onions over the hot side of the grill. Brown lightly on each side, then move the onions to the cold side of the grill. Close the lid on the grill.

Allow the meat to cook until it reaches desired doneness. Use an instant-read thermometer to determine the internal temperature of the meat (125 degrees for rare, 145 degrees for medium, and 160 degrees for well done).

Remove the meat to a clean plate. Cover lightly with aluminum foil and allow to rest for 10 minutes before carving. Remove the onions from each skewer and place them on a preheated platter.

To serve the steak and the onions:

Place the meat on a clean cutting board and carve into 4 equal portions. Shingle the meat over the onions and pour the meat juices from the plate over the sliced meat.

✳ **CHEF'S NOTE:** Use metal skewers when grilling, and you won't have to worry about the skewers burning. If you use bamboo skewers, make sure you soak them in water for 1 hour before using.

4 SERVINGS

BAKED NORTH ATLANTIC HALIBUT WITH A WILD MUSHROOM CRUST AND RAGOUT OF HARVEST VEGETABLES

To make the butternut squash puree needed in this recipe, peel and dice about 1 cup of squash. Place in a saucepan with enough water to cover. Bring to a boil and cook until soft. Drain and puree.

Mushroom Crust:

3 tablespoons unsalted butter

2 tablespoons shallots, peeled and finely chopped

1 teaspoon finely chopped garlic

2 cups assorted wild mushrooms, finely sliced

Salt and freshly ground black pepper, to taste

Sauce:

1/2 cup dry white wine

1/2 cup butternut squash puree

1/2 cup fish stock

1 sprig of fresh thyme

8 to 10 peppercorns

2 tablespoons unsalted butter

Salt and freshly ground black pepper, to taste

Ragout:

2 tablespoons unsalted butter

8 pearl onions, peeled

1/2 cup Macomber turnip, peeled and diced (parsnip or purple-top turnip may be used instead)

1/2 cup red Kuri squash, peeled and diced (Butternut or Acorn Squash may be used instead)

4 small red Bliss potatoes, cut into wedges and parboiled for 6 minutes

1 cup black Tuscan kale, ribs removed and chopped

Salt and freshly ground black pepper, to taste

Halibut:

4 (5-ounce) halibut fillets, skinless

Salt and freshly ground black pepper, to taste

1/4 cup pumpkin seeds, toasted brown, for garnish

2 tablespoons pumpkin seed oil, for garnish

To make the mushroom crust:

In a medium-size sauté pan over medium heat, melt the butter. Add the shallots, garlic and mushrooms. Sauté for about 4 minutes, being careful not to over stir as this will make the mushrooms give off excess moisture. Remove from the heat. Spread the mushroom mixture in an even layer on a cookie sheet to cool. Season to taste with salt and pepper. Set aside.

To make the sauce:

In a saucepan over medium-high heat, combine the wine, squash puree, fish stock, thyme and peppercorns. Bring to a boil. Lower the heat and simmer until reduced by one-third, about 6 to 8 minutes. Remove the pan from the heat and whisk in the butter. Season to taste with salt and pepper. Strain and keep warm.

To make the ragout:

In a medium-size pan over medium heat, melt the butter. Add the onions and cook, stirring occasionally, until translucent, about 4 to 5 minutes. Add the turnips and sauté for 2 minutes. Add the squash and potatoes. Stir occasionally until all the vegetables are cooked, about 3 minutes. Add the kale, tossing lightly until tender, about 1 minute. Season to taste with salt and pepper.

To bake the halibut:

Preheat oven to 425 degrees.

Lay the halibut fillets on a wax paper-lined cookie sheet. Season with salt and pepper. Divide the mushroom mixture equally, spreading to form an even layer on top of each fillet. Bake for about 7 minutes, or until the fish begins to turn white. Remove from the oven (the fish will continue to cook – overcooking will result in dry fish because halibut has a low fat content).

Divide the vegetable ragout equally on 4 plates. Place a fish fillet on the vegetables. Ladle the sauce around the fish. Garnish with pumpkin seeds and drizzle with pumpkin seed oil.

4 SERVINGS

✴ MOLASSES GLAZED GRILLED CHICKEN WING DRUMMETTES WITH GRILLED ASPARAGUS

Chicken wing drummettes, or lollipops, are a popular appetizer these days. The chicken wings may be scraped into their lollipop shape a day in advance. The accompanying glaze can be made a week in advance and used with other meats.

Chicken:

18 chicken wing drummettes, trimmed

1 teaspoon ground cumin

1 teaspoon chili powder

1 and ¹/₂ teaspoons salt

1 teaspoon freshly ground black pepper

Glaze:

¹/₄ cup molasses

¹/₂ cup barbecue sauce

2 tablespoons red wine vinegar

1 teaspoon salt

Asparagus:

2 pounds asparagus, medium-size, trimmed

2 tablespoons olive oil

Salt and freshly ground black pepper, to taste

To prepare the chicken drummettes:
While holding on to the narrow end of each chicken wing, slice through the skin in a circular motion to the bone with a paring or boning knife. Using the back of the knife, scrape the meat towards the thick end of the drummette. The drummette should now have the shape of a lollipop. Place the drummettes on a baking sheet lined with foil. Season the chicken drummettes with the cumin, chili powder, salt and pepper. Refrigerate.

To prepare the glaze:
In a medium-size mixing bowl, use a whisk to mix all the glaze ingredients. Reserve 1/4 cup of glaze for later use.

To grill the chicken drummettes:
Prepare the grill.

Grill the chicken drummettes on a well-oiled grill rack 5 to 6 inches from the source of heat for 4 to 5 minutes per side, or until light brown in color. Lower the heat or move the chicken to a cooler section of the grill. Using a brush, baste the chicken with the glaze. Continue to cook the chicken for 4 to 5 minutes, turning the drummettes and basting with more glaze until fully cooked and golden brown. Remove the chicken to a serving platter.

To grill the asparagus:
Place the asparagus on a baking sheet lined with aluminum foil. Brush or drizzle the asparagus with the olive oil. Season with salt and pepper. Place the asparagus on the hottest part of the grill. Cook for 3 minutes, then carefully rotate the asparagus with a metal pancake turner. Cook for 2 to 3 more minutes or until tender. Lay the asparagus next to the chicken drummettes on the serving platter. Drizzle the chicken with the reserved glaze.

4 TO 6 SERVINGS

→ PROSCIUTTO-WRAPPED BEEF TENDERLOIN WITH TRUFFLED FINGERLING POTATO-FILLED BABY PUMPKINS

This is a perfect dish for an autumn dinner party. Intensely flavored, elegant and colorful, it's sure to impress.

1 (24-ounce) barrel-cut beef tenderloin filet
1/2 cup heavy cream
1 teaspoon salt
1/2 teaspoon cracked black pepper
8 thin slices prosciutto
Salt and freshly ground black pepper, to taste

Vegetables:
4 baby pumpkins
1 tablespoon butter, at room temperature
Salt and freshly ground black pepper, to taste
8 fingerling potatoes
1 cup heavy cream
1 tablespoon cornstarch
3 tablespoons water
1/4 cup truffle oil
3 tablespoons truffle peelings (available in gourmet shops)
1 bunch broccoli rabe, blanched for 2 minutes

Sauce:
1 750ml bottle red wine
3 tablespoons honey
Salt and freshly ground black pepper, to taste

To prepare the beef tenderloin for roasting:
Place the tenderloin on a clean cutting board and carefully trim off 5 ounces (about 1 cup) of the beef lengthwise, keeping the tenderloin shaped like a cylinder. Place the trimmings in a food processor and chop finely. Pour in the cream and pulse for 10 seconds. Add the salt and pepper, and pulse again for 5 seconds. Remove mixture and place in a bowl.

Lay a 14-inch sheet of aluminum foil on a cutting board. Top with a 14-inch sheet of parchment or waxed paper. Lay the prosciutto slices on the paper overlapping inch to form a rectangle with a 1-inch border surrounding the paper. Spread the processed meat mixture evenly over the prosciutto to form a thin layer. Season the tenderloin with salt and pepper. Place the tenderloin on top of the meat mixture.

Roll up all the ingredients in the paper and foil, and twist the ends to tighten, making sure the cylinder shape is retained and it is completely covered by the foil. Place on a wire rack on a cookie sheet and refrigerate.

To prepare the vegetables:
Preheat oven to 400 degrees.

Wash and dry the baby pumpkins. Rub with butter. Season with salt and pepper. Place on a cookie sheet and bake for about 30 minutes, or until the edges of the pumpkins are lightly brown and the skin is easily pierced with a fork. Allow the pumpkins to cool. Slice off the tops of the pumpkins and set aside for later use. Scoop out the seeds.

Place the potatoes in a saucepan and cover with cold water. Bring to a boil and simmer until tender, about 5 minutes. Drain and place the potatoes on a cookie sheet to cool.

In a saucepan, bring the cream to a boil and then reduce to a simmer. In a bowl, combine the cornstarch with the 3 tablespoons of water. Slowly stir the cornstarch mixture into the cream. Continue stirring until the mixture returns to a boil and thickens, about 2 minutes. Remove from the heat and season with salt, pepper, truffle oil and truffle peelings. Cover and keep warm.

Roughly chop the broccoli rabe and set aside.

To make the sauce:

In a saucepan over medium-high heat, bring the red wine to a boil and allow to simmer until reduced to 1 cup, about 25 minutes. Pour reduction into a small bowl. Stir in the honey. Season with salt and pepper. Set aside, keeping the sauce warm.

To roast the beef tenderloin:

Preheat oven to 425 degrees.

Place the wrapped tenderloin in the oven for 20 minutes. Remove from the oven and allow to rest for 5 minutes.

During that time, place the pumpkins in the oven for about 5 minutes.

Add the potatoes and broccoli rabe to the truffle cream sauce. Bring to a boil. Remove from heat. Set aside.

Remove the foil and paper from the tenderloin.

To assemble each dinner plate:

Place a baby pumpkin on a plate and fill with the truffled potato and broccoli rabe mixture. Top with the reserved pumpkin cap. Slice the tenderloin into 4 equal portions and place a portion next to each pumpkin. Drizzle the plate with the wine sauce.

4 SERVINGS

⊹ CARAMELIZED CORIANDER DUCK BREASTS

These duck breasts should have an even coating of the coriander rub, not a heavy solid coating. Coriander has a nice spiciness, but too much of a good thing would be overdoing it.

4 prime boneless duck breasts

Marinade:
1/8 cup cognac
1/4 cup low-sodium soy sauce
1/2 cup pineapple juice
1/2 teaspoon finely chopped ginger root

Rub:
2 tablespoons crushed coriander seeds
1/2 teaspoon freshly ground black pepper
1 teaspoon kosher salt
1 teaspoon granulated sugar

Pan Sauce:
1/8 cup Grand Marnier
1/2 cup orange juice
1/4 cup brown veal stock
1/2 cup granulated sugar
1/4 ounce raspberry vinegar
1 teaspoon cornstarch mixed with 1/8 cup cold water
Zest from an orange, cut into very thin strips, poached

Garnish:
Fried pickled ginger (optional)*
*Available in large supermarkets

To marinate and sear the duck breasts:

Rinse the duck breasts and pat dry. With a very sharp knife, score the skin in a 1/2-inch diamond pattern, being careful to cut only through the skin, not into the meat.

Combine the marinade ingredients. Place the duck breasts in the marinade for 30 minutes, turning them over occasionally to provide even steeping.

Combine the rub ingredients. Remove the duck breasts from the marinade and pat dry. Coat with the rub ingredients, pushing the rub into the duck on both sides.

Preheat oven to 450 degrees.

Place a heavy-bottomed sauté pan, preferably with a stainless steel surface, over medium-high heat, and allow the pan to become very hot. Place the duck breasts skin side down. They should immediately start to sizzle and release the fats contained in the skin. Continue to cook the duck breasts, rendering the fat and being careful not to burn the breasts. Remove excess fat from the pan while cooking the breasts, which should have a nicely browned surface in 7 to 8 minutes. When the skin is dark brown and all the fat has been removed from the pan, turn the breasts over and sear the meat side for about 2 minutes. The meat will still be very rare.

Remove the breasts from the sauté pan, and place them in a roasting pan, meat side down. Place the pan in the oven for 8 to 10 minutes. Remove the pan from the oven, pour off the fat, and immediately place the breasts on a serving platter, skin side down. Allow the breasts to rest for 3 to 4 minutes in a warm place.

To make the sauce:

Deglaze the pan by adding the Grand Marnier and scraping up the browned bits with a whisk or fork. Place the pan over medium heat. Add the orange juice and brown veal stock, stirring constantly. This rustic-style sauce can be served as it is, or it can be strained for a more refined sauce.

In a flat-bottomed pan over high heat, melt the sugar. The sugar will turn into a clear liquid and then quickly begin to brown. As it approaches its caramelized state, continue to stir the melted sugar which will begin to foam lightly with tiny bubbles, creating a ruby-brown coloring. Quickly remove the pan from the heat and add the raspberry vinegar to stop the caramelization process and stabilize the color. Add the pan sauce to the caramelized sugar. Bring to a boil. Adjust the thickness of the sauce by adding the cornstarch and water mixture (known as a slurry), stirring to give body to the sauce. Add the poached orange zest.

To serve the duck breasts:

Slice each duck breast on the bias and fan out on a dinner plate, skin side up. Drizzle the sauce lightly along the inside rim of the plate. Garnish with fried pickled ginger, if desired.

4 SERVINGS

⟶ VEGETABLE-CITRUS COUSCOUS

Instant couscous turns into something quite special with the added flavors of fresh vegetables and fruit juices.

3 tablespoons olive oil

2 garlic cloves, minced

¹/₂ cup chopped scallions

¹/₂ cup diced zucchini

¹/₂ cup diced carrots

¹/₂ cup diced red bell pepper

1 cup sliced mushrooms (cremini, button, shiitake or a combination)

2 tablespoons lime juice

¹/₄ cup orange juice

2 and ¹/₂ cups chicken stock

3 tablespoons unsalted butter

1 teaspoon ground cinnamon

Kosher salt, as needed

2 cups instant couscous

¹/₂ cup diced, peeled and seeded cucumber

Freshly ground black pepper, to taste

To cook the vegetables:

In a large skillet, heat 1 tablespoon olive oil over medium-high heat. Add half the garlic and all the scallions, zucchini, carrots and peppers. Cook, stirring often, for about 3 minutes, or until the vegetables are softened but still firm. Transfer the vegetables to a bowl. Set aside. Wipe the skillet clean.

To cook the mushrooms:

Heat the remaining olive oil in the skillet over high heat. Add the remaining garlic and all the mushrooms. Cook, stirring often, until any liquid has been cooked off and the mushrooms are softened and beginning to brown around the edges. Transfer garlic-mushroom mixture to a bowl. Set aside.

To cook the couscous:

In a medium-size saucepan with a tight-fitting lid, bring the lime juice, orange juice, chicken stock, butter, cinnamon and 1 teaspoon salt to a boil. Stir in the couscous. Cover and turn off the heat. Let rest for 10 minutes to absorb the liquid, then gently fold in the cooked vegetables, mushrooms and cucumber. Keep tightly covered until ready to serve. Before serving, fluff with a fork and season to taste with salt and pepper.

6 SERVINGS

✧ CHICKEN POT ROAST

You've heard of beef pot roast, and now there's a light alternative chicken pot roast, perfectly seasoned with fresh herbs.

5 to 6 pounds cut-up chicken (legs, thighs and breasts)
Salt and freshly ground black pepper, to taste
2 tablespoons olive oil
2 cups diced napa cabbage
1 and $^{1}/_{2}$ cups diced carrots
1 and $^{1}/_{2}$ cups diced onions
1 and $^{1}/_{2}$ cups diced Yukon gold potatoes
2 quarts chicken stock (8 cups)
$^{1}/_{4}$ cup chopped parsley
2 tablespoons chopped fresh thyme
2 tablespoons chopped fresh rosemary

To prepare the chicken:
Season the chicken with salt and pepper. Heat the olive oil in a large saucepan. Brown the chicken pieces on all sides. Remove the chicken from the pan and discard the oil.

To prepare the vegetables:
Return the chicken thighs and legs to the pan along with the diced vegetables and chicken stock. Over medium-high heat, bring the stock to a boil and simmer for about 45 minutes, until the chicken and vegetables are very tender. Add the chicken breasts and simmer for an additional 20 minutes.

To serve the chicken and vegetables:
Using a slotted spoon, remove the chicken and vegetables from the stock. Arrange on a serving platter. Drizzle some of the stock over the platter. Sprinkle with fresh herbs just before serving.

8 SERVINGS

⤞ SALMON ROASTED IN GRAPEVINE LEAVES, GRAPE AND GRAIN SALAD WITH VERJUS VINAIGRETTE

This is a very elegant dinner entrée that sounds a lot more complicated than it is to prepare. It will surely impress your dinner guests. If rye berries or wheat berries are not available, you may substitute a mixture of grains, such as beluga or baby lentils or barley.

8 (4-ounce) salmon fillets, all approximately
  1-inch thick
Salt and freshly ground black pepper, to taste
8 to 16 pickled grapevine leaves, depending on size*
1 tablespoon minced ginger
1 tablespoon minced garlic
1 tablespoon curry powder
1 tablespoon Dijon mustard
5 to 7 drops Tabasco
4 very thin slices lemon, each cut into pie shapes
1 tablespoon olive oil
verjus vinaigrette (recipe follows)

Salad:
1 cup rye berries or wheat berries, cooked until tender in 3 to 4 cups water
1 cup julienned carrots
1 cup assorted seedless grapes: champagne, green, red (large ones cut in half)
1 cup Italian parsley, roughly chopped or torn
1 tablespoon minced or grated lemon zest
3 to 4 tablespoons roughly chopped fresh tarragon
³/4 cup verjus vinaigrette

Garnish: Curry, mustard or basil oil, as needed

* Available in Middle Eastern markets

To prepare the salmon:

Season the fish lightly with salt and pepper, remembering that the grapevine leaves are packed in salted brine.

Mix the ginger, garlic, curry powder, mustard and Tabasco into a paste, and smear evenly over the top of the salmon filets. Top each piece of salmon with a piece of lemon. Lay the grapevine leaves smooth side down on a clean counter or cutting board. Place the salmon lemon side down on the leaves and wrap each leaf around the salmon, making sure that the fish is completely covered. If the leaves are too small, use 2 leaves. The salmon can be prepared to this point up to a day in advance and covered and stored in the refrigerator.

To bake the salmon:

Preheat oven to 550 degrees.

Rub each salmon package with a little olive oil. Quickly sauté the salmon packages on top of the stove in a skillet. The grapevine leaves on both sides of the salmon packages should be lightly colored.

Place the salmon packages on a baking sheet. Sprinkle with the verjus vinaigrette and place on the top rack of the oven. Cook 8 (medium-rare) to 10 (medium-well) minutes. The salmon should have an internal temperature of at least 130 degrees. It will continue to cook once it is removed from the oven (this is called carry-over cooking).

To make the salad:

While the salmon is cooking, toss together the ingredients for the salad and season to taste with salt and pepper.

To serve the salmon and salad:

Spoon some of the salad onto the middle of each plate and top with the salmon package. Garnish with a little curry, mustard or basil oil. Offer additional verjus vinaigrette on the side.

Each package may be torn open at the top for easy access to the salmon and to show the pink interior.

✳ **CHEF'S NOTE:** All grains have different cooking times. They should be brought to the boil in unsalted water (salt will toughen the grains) and then reduced to a simmer. Wheat berries and barley should take 30 minutes to become tender. Lentils take less time, 10 to 15 minutes.

8 SERVINGS

Verjus Vinaigrette

1 cup verjus or white grape juice

2 tablespoons lemon juice

1 cup extra virgin olive oil

1 teaspoon minced garlic

Salt and freshly ground black pepper, to taste

To make the vinaigrette:

Combine all the ingredients. Mix well. Store in a squeeze bottle, if desired.

✳ **CHEF'S NOTE:** When selecting Italian parsley at the market, choose bunches with smaller, more tender leaves.

MAKES 2 CUPS

→ SWORDFISH WITH BRAISED FENNEL, TOMATOES AND CAPERS

Anyone who enjoys swordfish will appreciate this version with its unusual salty and sweet sauce made with olives, capers and raisins.

Marinade:
$^1/_2$ cup olive oil

2 garlic cloves, minced

$^1/_4$ teaspoon freshly ground black pepper

1 tablespoon chopped fresh dill or fennel fronds

Grated zest from 1 orange

2 tablespoons dry red wine

$^1/_4$ teaspoon crushed fennel seeds

$^1/_2$ teaspoon red pepper flakes (optional)

Fish:
4 swordfish steaks, at least 1-inch thick, about 7 ounces each

Vegetables:
4 garlic cloves, minced

2 shallots, minced

$^1/_2$ cup olive oil

1 teaspoon fresh thyme leaves

Kosher salt and freshly ground black pepper, to taste

3 large beefsteak tomatoes, cored and cut into quarters

2 medium-size fennel bulbs, cut into quarters

$^1/_2$ to 1 cup chicken stock

2 tablespoons green olives, pitted and cut in half

2 tablespoons black olives, pitted and cut in half

2 tablespoons small capers in vinegar, drained

$^1/_4$ cup golden raisins

2 tablespoons cold unsalted butter

1 tablespoon chopped cilantro

Garnish:
Fresh cilantro

$^1/_4$ cup toasted pine nuts

Lemon wedges, as needed

To marinate the swordfish:

In a bowl, whisk together the marinade ingredients. Arrange the fish in a single layer in a large glass or ceramic baking dish. Pour the marinade over the fish. Turn to coat the fish. Cover with plastic wrap and refrigerate for at least 2 hours, preferably overnight.

To braise the vegetables:

Preheat the oven to 350 degrees.

In a large bowl, toss the garlic and shallots with the olive oil. Add the thyme, salt, pepper, tomatoes and fennel. Toss gently to coat well. On a baking sheet with sides, arrange the tomato quarters cut side down. Arrange the fennel around the tomatoes. Pour $^1/_2$ cup chicken stock into the pan. Cover the pan with aluminum foil. Bake for 30 to 40 minutes. Uncover the pan and bake an additional 10 minutes. Remove the tomatoes and fennel from the pan; place in an oven-proof baking dish and keep warm in the turned-off oven.

To make the sauce:
Transfer the juices and seasonings remaining on the baking sheet to a saucepan. Bring to a boil, adding more chicken stock if needed to keep the mixture moist. Stir in the olives, capers and raisins. Whisk in the butter. Stir in the cilantro. Season again with salt and pepper.

To grill or broil the swordfish:
Prepare the grill or oven broiler until very hot. Remove the fish from the marinade and drain briefly. Discard the marinade. Season the fish on both sides with salt and pepper. Grill or broil 2 to 3 minutes on each side, or longer if desired.

To serve the swordfish and vegetables:
Place a tomato quarter and a fennel quarter on each dinner plate. Rest the fish on top of the tomato and fennel. Spoon the sauce on top of the fish. Sprinkle with cilantro and pine nuts. Serve immediately with lemon wedges.

4 SERVINGS

✣ HARVEST QUAIL WITH ROASTED ZINFANDEL SAUCE

This dish can be prepared as an appetizer course or as a main entrée. For an appetizer, one quail per person would suffice. As an entrée, two quail would be ample with side dishes.

4 boneless quail
Salt and freshly ground black pepper, to taste

Stuffing:
1 teaspoon chopped shallots
¼ teaspoon minced roasted garlic
1 teaspoon chopped parsley
½ cup boneless chicken, duck or pork (or a combination)
⅛ cup cognac
Salt and freshly ground black pepper, to taste
4 ounces fresh French bread
¼ cup dried cranberries, reconstituted and chopped
¼ cup dried apricots, reconstituted and chopped
Pinch of thyme
All-purpose flour, as needed, seasoned with salt,
  pepper and a pinch of thyme
Olive oil, as needed

Zinfandel Sauce:
1 teaspoon chopped shallots
½ teaspoon chopped roasted garlic
2 bay leaves
⅛ cup cognac
1 and ½ cups red Zinfandel
½ cup brown veal stock
1 tablespoon red currant jelly

To prepare the stuffing:
In a food processor, combine the shallots, garlic, parsley and meat. Purée the mixture. Add the cognac, salt and pepper, and blend. Add the fresh bread, blending well. Add the chopped fruits and thyme, pulsing to blend. Do not over process.

To prepare the quail:
Rinse the quail and pat dry. Season the quail inside and out with salt and pepper. Stuff the cavity of each quail with the stuffing. Fold the legs of the quail in to help retain its plump natural shape.

To cook the quail:
Preheat oven to 375 degrees.

Place a large ovenproof sauté pan over medium-high heat. Lightly flour the quail. Add a minimal amount of oil to the sauté pan. Sauté the quail, breast side down, until golden brown. Turn and brown on both sides. Remove the pan from the heat. Transfer the quail to a warm roasting platter. Pour off excess oil and fat from the pan.

To prepare the sauce:
Return the pan to the stove, and lower the heat to medium-low. Add the shallots and garlic. Sauté quickly. Add the bay leaves and cognac, being careful because the alcohol in the cognac may flame. Scrape the bottom of the pan to blend in any residue for a flavorful sauce. Add the wine, blending well. Place the quail in the pan. Add the brown veal stock and raise the heat, bringing the mixture

to a simmer. Move the pan into the oven and roast for 20 to 25 minutes.

Remove the pan from the oven. Place the quail on a warm roasting platter and keep warm. Strain the sauce and adjust the seasoning, if necessary. Place the quail on a serving plate. Spoon the sauce over each quail.

✳ **CHEF'S NOTE:** Recommended accompaniments are roasted fall vegetables, wild rice cakes, sautéed winter kale and a cranberry relish garnish. To make the sauce, use a high-quality red Zinfandel

4 SERVINGS

✦ PORK TENDERLOIN STUFFED WITH PROSCIUTTO AND GRILLED VEGETABLES

An unusual stuffing made of grilled vegetables and Mediterranean spices elevates this pork dish to new heights.

Stuffing:

1 large portabello mushroom cap

¹/₂ yellow pepper

¹/₂ red pepper

Salt and freshly ground black pepper, to taste

¹/₄ cup diced provolone cheese

2 tablespoons minced prosciutto

¹/₂ teaspoon lemon zest

2 tablespoons roughly chopped Italian parsley

¹/₂ teaspoon oregano

¹/₂ teaspoon basil

¹/₂ teaspoon thyme

¹/₂ teaspoon chopped garlic

1 large pork tenderloin (1 to 1 and ¹/₂ pounds)

3-4 slices prosciutto

Oil, as needed

To grill the vegetables:

Prepare the grill. Over medium-high heat, quickly grill the vegetables. Remove the skin from the peppers. Season the vegetables with salt and pepper. Dice the vegetables. Toss the vegetables with the cheese, prosciutto, lemon zest, herbs and spices. Season to taste with more salt and pepper, if needed.

To prepare the pork:

Cut the pork into 4 equal portions. Cut a pocket into each pork medallion. Stuff each pocket with as much filling as possible. Cover each stuffed pocket with a piece of prosciutto. Tie with butcher's twine.

Preheat oven to 400 degrees.

In a hot skillet, sear the pork medallions on all sides in oil. Place the pork medallions in the oven and roast for 10 to 15 minutes. Remove from oven. Allow to rest for 5 minutes. Slice and serve.

❋ **CHEF'S NOTE:** To prepare the tenderloin whole, take a sharpened steel covered in plastic wrap and gently insert it down the middle of the tenderloin, using a back and forth motion to enlarge the pocket. After stuffing, cover the opening (and any holes that may have been made) with prosciutto.

Sear as directed, then roast at 400 degrees for 25 to 30 minutes.

2 TO 4 SERVINGS

RUSSIA

→ STUFFED CABBAGE ROLLS

The most widely used cabbage comes in compact heads of waxy, tightly wrapped leaves that range in color from almost white to green to red. Choose a cabbage with fresh, crisp-looking leaves that are firmly packed. The head should be heavy for its size. Cabbage can be refrigerated tightly wrapped for about a week.

1 head green cabbage

Stuffing:
2 tablespoons oil
1 cup diced onions
1/2 pound lean ground beef
1/2 pound ground turkey
1 cup cooked rice
1/2 cup finely diced Swiss cheese
2 eggs
Salt and freshly ground black pepper, to taste
1/4 cup chopped parsley
6 sun-dried yellow tomatoes, chopped

1 quart chicken stock
2 tablespoons oil
2 leeks, white part only, cut into thin julienne strips
1/2 cup sliced mushrooms
1 green pepper, diced
4 plum tomatoes, diced

1/3 cup Madeira wine

To prepare the cabbage leaves:
Remove the outer leaves from the head of cabbage. Remove the core. In a stockpot of boiling salted water, blanch the head of cabbage, removing leaves as they become tender. Place the leaves on a shallow tray. Trim the leaves, if necessary.

To make the stuffing:
In a large sauté pan, heat the oil. Sauté the onions in the oil until wilted. Allow to cool.

Combine all remaining ingredients for the stuffing. Place a small amount of stuffing on each cabbage leaf and roll up. Place the cabbage rolls stem side down in a shallow braising pan.

Bring chicken stock to a boil. Pour stock over cabbage rolls, almost covering them. (You may not need the entire quart of stock.) Bring to a boil over medium-high heat. Cover the pan with a lid. Reduce to a simmer and cook for 45 minutes.

To make the sauce:
In another sauté pan, heat the oil. Sauté the leeks, mushrooms, peppers and tomatoes until wilted. Pour this mixture over the cabbage rolls. Deglaze the pan with the Madeira wine. Add this to the cabbage rolls. Simmer an additional 15 to 20 minutes. Serve the cabbage rolls and sauce topped with sour cream, if desired.

4 TO 6 SERVINGS

☙ MOTHER-IN-LAW CAKE

This cake is reserved for special occasions in Russia. It is delicious and rich yet not overwhelming with sweetness. It is a traditional recipe passed down from generation to generation.

Cake Layers:

1 and ³/4 sticks butter

5 tablespoons sugar

¹/₂ teaspoon salt

1 cup walnuts, ground

2 tablespoons sour cream

2 cups flour

Filling:

4 tablespoons butter

¹/₄ cup sugar

¹/₂ teaspoon vanilla

¹/₄ cup sour cream

¹/₄ cup walnuts, toasted and chopped

1 tablespoon cognac

Chocolate Glaze:

2 tablespoons milk

¹/₄ cup sugar

1 teaspoon cocoa powder

1 tablespoon butter

To make the cake layers:
Preheat oven to 350 degrees.

In a large bowl, blend together the butter, sugar and salt. Add the ground walnuts and sour cream; mix well. Slowly add the flour until completely incorporated.

Pipe or pat out 4 rounds, each about 8 inches in diameter, on a baking sheet. Bake for 15 minutes. Allow to cool completely.

To make the filling:
In a separate bowl, cream the butter and sugar until completely blended. Gradually stir in the remaining ingredients. Chill in the refrigerator for 10 minutes. Spread the chilled filling evenly between the stacked cake layers.

To make the chocolate glaze:
In a small saucepan, bring the milk, sugar and cocoa powder to a boil. Remove from heat and stir in butter. After the glaze thickens a bit, spread it over the top layer of the cake. Chill in the refrigerator for several hours before serving.

12 SERVINGS

INDIA

⤳ ROGHAN GHOSHT (LAMB IN YOGURT)

Many spices flavor this dish. Long, slow cooking results in tender bites of lamb in an exotic sauce. This is a variation on a traditional Indian recipe. It has been altered slightly to suit the American palate.

4 tablespoons oil
1 and ¹/2 pounds lean lamb, cubed
2 onions, minced
1 tablespoon paprika*
1 cup plain yogurt

Paste:
2 garlic cloves, peeled
1-inch piece fresh ginger
2 green chilies, fresh
1 tablespoon coriander seeds
1 teaspoon cumin
1 teaspoon fresh mint, chopped
1 teaspoon fresh cilantro, chopped
2 to 3 tablespoons plain yogurt

6 cardamom pods (lightly crushed)
6 cloves
1-inch cinnamon stick
Salt, as needed
1 cup slivered almonds

To prepare the lamb:
In a large frying pan, heat 2 tablespoons of oil. Add the lamb and brown on all sides. Remove the lamb from the pan and set aside. Add half the onions and the paprika; sauté until the onions become soft. Return the lamb to the pan. Add the yogurt, stir-ring well. Cover and simmer for 20 minutes.

*If you would like this dish to be hotter, sub-stitute 1 teaspoon of cayenne pepper for the paprika.

To make the paste:
In a food processor, combine the garlic, ginger, chilies, coriander seeds, cumin, mint, cilantro and 2 to 3 tablespoons yogurt. Blend until mixture becomes a smooth paste. Set aside.

To complete the dish:
In a large heavy pan, heat the remaining oil. Add the cardamom pods, cloves and cinnamon stick. Cook for 1 minute. Add the remaining onions and prepared paste. Cook for 5 minutes, stirring con-stantly.

Add the lamb mixture. Season to taste with salt. Stir well and bring to a simmer. Cover and cook for 30 minutes. Add almonds and cook for an addi-tional 15 minutes or until tender.

✳ **CHEF'S NOTE:** Cardamom is a member of the ginger family and native to India. Cardamom seeds are encapsulated in small pods about the size of a cranberry. Each pod contains about 20 tiny seeds. If using cardamom to flavor dishes, lightly crush the shell of the pod and add the pods and seeds to the mixture. The shell will disintegrate while the dish cooks.

6 SERVINGS

→ PURI STUFFED WITH DHAL

Puri, also known as poori, is a deep-fried bread that is round, flat and unleavened. It's made with whole-wheat flour, water and ghee (clarified butter). Dhal, also known as dal, is a spicy dish made with lentils, tomatoes, onions and various seasonings.

1 cup dried black beans

1 fresh green chili, chopped

¹/₂ teaspoon salt

1 tablespoon anise seed

1 teaspoon coriander seed

¹/₂ teaspoon cumin seed

¹/₂ teaspoon red chili powder

¹/₄ teaspoon asafetida powder (available in Indian specialty markets)

4 and ¹/₂ cups all-purpose flour

1 cup warm water, as needed

Vegetable oil, as needed for frying

Fresh cilantro, as needed for garnish

To prepare the dhal:

Soak black beans in water overnight. Rinse in cold water and drain well.

In a food processor, grind the black beans with the green chili, salt and all spices.

To make the dough:

In a large bowl, sift the flour and gradually add just enough water to make a soft dough. Knead until smooth; cover with a damp cloth and allow to rest for 45 minutes.

To make the puri:

Divide the dough into 16 equal portions. Roll into balls, then flatten into 2-inch disks. Place an equal portion of stuffing in the center of each piece of dough; Fold in half and pinch the dough to seal in the stuffing. Gently flatten the stuffed puri by hand or with a rolling pin.

Heat the oil to 350 degrees for deep-frying. Fry the balls of dough until golden brown. Remove the puri from the oil and place on screen or rack to drain off excess oil. Place puri on serving plate, garnished with fresh cilantro. For additional flavor, you may serve the puri with mint or coriander chutney, available in Indian and gourmet markets.

8 SERVINGS

IRELAND

POTATO-CRUSTED FILLETS OF SALMON WITH CABBAGE SLAW AND BAILEY'S IRISH CREAM REDUCTION

This potato-encrusted salmon dish makes quite an impression at dinner parties and proves that gourmet food is alive and well in Ireland.

4 tablespoons olive oil, divided

4 cups green cabbage, shredded

1 medium carrot, peeled and grated

1 medium zucchini, peeled and grated

1 teaspoon malt vinegar

Salt and freshly ground black pepper, to taste

4 (8-ounce) salmon fillets

2 tablespoons whole-grain mustard, reserving

½ teaspoon for sauce

1 large Idaho potato, peeled and cut into thin julienne strips

2 teaspoons butter

1 tablespoon shallots, peeled and finely diced

2 cups heavy cream

1/4 cup Bailey's Irish Cream

To prepare the cabbage slaw:

Preheat the oven to 350 degrees.

Place 2 tablespoons of oil in a sauté pan and add the cabbage. Over medium-high heat, cook until the cabbage is limp, about 5 to 10 minutes. Add the carrots and zucchini; continue to cook for 2 minutes. Add the vinegar; season with salt and pepper. Remove from heat and place in the oven.

To prepare the salmon:

Coat one side of each salmon fillet with mustard. Coat that same side of each fillet with the thin julienne strips of potato. In a large skillet, heat the remaining olive oil. Place the fillets, potato side down, in the pan. Over high heat, sear the fillets 2 minutes on each side. Remove the fillets from the pan, place them in an oven-proof dish, and bake in the oven with the cabbage slaw for 20 minutes.

Wipe the skillet clean. Add the butter and shallots. Over medium-high heat, sauté lightly. Add the heavy cream and Bailey's Irish Cream. Reduce until sauce thickens. Add ½ teaspoon mustard. Season with salt and pepper.

To present and serve:

Place a generous serving of cabbage slaw in the center of each serving plate. Top with the salmon fillets, potato side up, and spoon the sauce around the outside of the slaw.

4 SERVINGS

⊹ ROASTED RACK OF LAMB WITH HERB CRUST AND MINT BUTTER SAUCE

Because of its delicate flavor, lamb is usually cooked as simply as possible. Lamb cooked medium-rare will be tender and succulent. Overcooking lamb makes it dry and tough.

1 (2-pound) rack of lamb, trimmed and Frenched
1 garlic clove, crushed
1 rosemary sprig, chopped
¼ teaspoon salt
¼ teaspoon freshly ground black pepper
1 tablespoon olive oil
4 tablespoons butter
1 teaspoon chopped parsley
½ teaspoon chopped tarragon
¼ teaspoon chopped basil
2 tablespoons tomatoes, skinned, seeded and roughly chopped
1 cup fresh breadcrumbs
1 and ½ cups chicken stock
1 teaspoon arrowroot

Sauce:
2 tablespoons tarragon vinegar
1 tablespoon lemon juice
1 bay leaf
¼ cup water
2 egg yolks
½ cup butter
6 mint leaves, finely chopped

To roast the rack of lamb:
Preheat oven to 350 degrees.

Rub the outside of the lamb rack with crushed garlic; sprinkle with rosemary, salt and pepper.

Cover the exposed bones with aluminum foi. Place in a roasting pan coated with the olive oil. Roast for 20 minutes, or until the lamb reaches an internal temperature of 140 degrees.

To make the herb crust:
In a small saucepan over medium heat, melt the butter. Mix in the herbs and chopped tomatoes. Add the breadcrumbs and mix until moist. Spread the breadcrumb mixture over the lamb. Return the lamb to the oven and roast for another 5 minutes. Allow to rest in a warm place.

To make gravy:
Pour off the excess fat from the roasting pan. Deglaze the pan with chicken stock. Mix the arrowroot with 1 teaspoon of stock, add to the pan to thicken the juices. Strain and set aside.

To make the mint-butter sauce:
In a small saucepan over medium-high heat, combine the vinegar, lemon juice, bay leaf and water. Reduce to 2 tablespoons. Remove the bay leaf. Place the warm reduction in a food processor. Add the egg yolks. Blend at high speed until the egg yolks thicken, about 30 seconds.

Heat the butter to 120 degrees and slowly pour into the food processor set on high speed. Process for 2 minutes. Add the chopped mint leaves and mix well before serving.

2 SERVINGS

→ VEAL ESCALOPES WITH ORANGE BUTTER AND ROASTED VEGETABLE SALAD

Veal cutlets are more commonly known as escalopes in Ireland. Veal must be cooked very gently. Moist cooking methods are the most appropriate. Breading the cutlets helps seal in the veal's precious moisture. The delicate flavor of veal can easily be overpowered by strongly flavored sauces.

Roasted Vegetable Salad:

$^1/_2$ *cup thickly sliced carrots*

$^1/_2$ *cup thickly sliced parsnips*

$^1/_2$ *cup thickly sliced Jerusalem artichokes*

1 cup rutabaga, peeled and diced

$^1/_2$ *cup diced onion*

3 garlic cloves, crushed

2 tablespoons olive oil

$^1/_4$ *teaspoon salt*

$^1/_2$ *teaspoon freshly ground black pepper*

1 cup basic vinaigrette dressing (recipe follows)

Veal:

4 (2-ounce) veal cutlets, pounded flat

Salt and freshly ground black pepper

2 eggs

1 teaspoon chopped basil

1 teaspoon chopped thyme

2 tablespoons grated cheddar cheese

2 garlic cloves, crushed

6 tablespoons all-purpose flour

1 and cups fresh white breadcrumbs

1 cup safflower oil

4 tablespoons butter

Juice of 1 orange

2 oranges, peeled, pith removed, and cut into segments

1 grapefruit, peeled, pith removed, and cut into segments

1 cup mixed salad greens

To roast the vegetables:

Preheat oven to 400 degrees.

Place the prepared vegetables and garlic, with the olive oil and seasonings, in an ovenproof heavy-bottomed skillet. Over high heat, shake and toss the vegetables to make sure that they are well coated with the oil.

Place in the oven. Roast the vegetables for 15 minutes, or until they are caramelized and soft but firm. Remove from oven. Allow to cool.

When the vegetables are cool, toss them gently with the vinaigrette dressing. Refrigerate.

To prepare the veal:

Season the veal cutlets with salt and pepper.

In a bowl, beat the eggs. Add the herbs, cheese and garlic.

Dredge the cutlets in flour, then dip in the herbed egg and cheese mixture. Coat with breadcrumbs. Gently pat the breaded veal, cover and refrigerate for 30 minutes.

Heat the oil in a large, heavy-bottomed skillet. Place the cutlets in the oil and fry over moderate heat until golden brown on both sides. Remove the cutlets from the pan and set on paper towels to drain excess oil. Keep warm.

To make the orange butter:

In a separate saucepan, melt the butter. Add the orange juice and simmer until lightly browned.

To serve the veal escalopes:

Place a veal cutlet on a dinner plate. Coat with the orange butter and garnish with orange and grapefruit segments. Serve with the roasted vegetables and mixed salad greens.

Basic Vinaigrette

¹/₄ cup wine vinegar

Salt and freshly ground black pepper, to taste

³/₄ cup olive oil

Place the vinegar in a mixing bowl. Add salt and pepper. Gradually whisk in the oil until it forms an emulsion, or blend these ingredients in a food processor for 20 seconds. Place vinaigrette in squeeze bottle, if desired. Shake before use.

CHEF'S NOTE: Proportions of oil and vinegar may be adjusted to personal taste. Keep in mind that the strength of vinegars varies from one brand to another.

4 SERVINGS

⤸ CHOCOLATE ORANGE STOUT CAKE

Stout is a strong, dark beer that comes from the British Isles. It is made with barley which gives it a deep, dark color and bittersweet flavor. It adds an unusual richness to this citrus-tinged chocolate cake.

2 and ¹/₄ cups self-rising flour

1 teaspoon baking powder

¹/₄ teaspoon salt

3 tablespoons cocoa powder

¹/₂ pound unsalted butter, softened (2 sticks)

1 cup dark brown sugar

4 whole eggs

Grated zest from 1 whole orange

¹/₂ cup stout beer

To make the cake:

Preheat oven to 375 degrees.

Spray 2 (9-inch) cake pans with non-stick cooking spray and dust with flour.

Sift the flour, baking soda, salt and cocoa together; set aside.

Cream together the butter and sugar until light in color. Add the eggs one at a time; be sure they incorporate well before adding the next egg. Add the orange zest; mix to incorporate. Alternately add the sifted dry ingredients and the stout beginning and ending with dry ingredients.

Divide the batter equally between the 2 pans and bake for 30 to 40 minutes. The cake should spring back when touched and pull away from the sides of the pan. Allow to cool for 10 minutes and then remove from pans onto a cooling rack.

Icing

12 ounces unsalted butter, softened (3 sticks)

6 cups powdered sugar

Zest and juice from 1 whole orange

To make the icing:

While the cakes are cooling make the icing. Cream the butter and sugar together until light and fluffy. Add the zest and enough juice to make the icing soft enough to spread.

Once the cakes are cooled completely, start assembling. Place a third of the icing on the first layer and spread it as evenly as possible. Place the second layer on top and put another third of the icing on top of that layer. Finish the cake by using the last third of the icing to spread on the sides.

⤸ **CHEF'S NOTE:** This recipe calls for self-rising flour which is pre-sifted, so there is no need to sift the flour in this cake recipe. After spraying the cake pans with non-stick cooking spray, coat the pans with flour, tapping out any excess. This will prevent the baked layers from sticking to the pans.

ONE 9-INCH, 2-LAYER CAKE

MIDDLE EAST

✢ GRILLED GAME HENS CHERMOULA

Chermoula is a powerful puree that is used in Morocco as a marinade and dipping sauce for poultry and fish steaks such as tuna and swordfish. Here it is used to add a robust flavor to tender game hens on the grill.

Chermoula:

½ bunch cilantro

1 bunch flat leaf parsley

2 teaspoons whole cumin seeds, toasted and ground

1 teaspoon jalapeno chili pepper, seeded and minced

2 teaspoons sweet paprika

4 garlic cloves, peeled

3 tablespoons fresh lemon juice

2 tablespoons olive oil

1 teaspoon salt

2 Cornish game hens

1 pinch saffron

3 plum tomatoes, peeled, seeded and diced

½ cup chicken stock, heated

To make the Chermoula:

In a food processor, combine all the Chermoula ingredients and pulse until it becomes a coarse purée. Reserve ⅓ cup of the purée to use for the sauce.

To butterfly the game hens for grilling:

Turn each hen breast down and cut along the backbone from the neck to the tail end. Cut out the backbone, remove the wishbone and discard. Turn the game hen breast side up and flatten it with your hand to form a butterfly shape.

With your fingers, separate the skin from the flesh of the game hen and spread the remaining Chermoula purée between the flesh and skin. Cover and refrigerate for at least 2 hours.

Preheat the grill to medium heat. Place the game hens on the grill skin side down. Cook for 10 to 12 minutes or until golden brown. Turn the game hens and grill skin side up until the juices run clear, another 10 to 12 minutes. The internal temperature of the game hens should be 165 degrees.

To make the sauce:

In a saucepan, combine the reserved Chermoula purée with the saffron, tomatoes and chicken stock. Bring to a boil and drizzle over the game hens at serving time.

✳ **CHEF'S NOTE:** For a lower-fat version, the purée can be used with boneless skinless chicken breast, in which case the cooking time would be cut in half. This dish is also wonderful when served at room temperature or cold.

4 SERVINGS

✛ GRILLED FENNEL WITH ORANGE DRESSING

Fennel is used throughout the Mediterranean. It is often mislabeled as sweet anise. Fennel has a milder licorice flavor and a celery-like texture. It blends well with the citrus flavors of the dressing. This makes a great side dish with grilled meats.

¼ cup orange juice

1 tablespoon lemon juice

1 teaspoon grated orange peel

1 tablespoon minced shallots

Kosher or sea salt and freshly ground black pepper, to taste

2 large fennel bulbs

2 tablespoons olive oil

To make the dressing:
Combine the orange juice, lemon juice, grated orange peel, shallots, salt and pepper. Set aside.

To prepare the fennel:
Slice 1/4-inch off the root end of each fennel bulb. Trim the stalks and the feathery fronds of the bulbs, reserving a few fronds for garnish. Lay each fennel bulb on its side. With a large knife, cut the fennel into 1/2-inch thick slices through its core, which will hold most of the fennel together while grilling (don't worry if the fennel falls apart in large pieces).

Preheat the grill to medium-high heat. Toss the fennel with the olive oil. Grill the fennel on each side until tender and the surface begins to caramelize, 3 to 4 minutes per side. Remove from the grill and drizzle with the orange dressing.

4 SERVINGS

HEALTHY

→ SOBA NOODLES WITH MARINATED VEGETABLES

Soba is a Japanese noodle made from buckwheat and wheat flour which gives it a dark brownish-gray color. Soba noodles are available in natural food stores and in the Asian section of large supermarkets.

1 pound soba noodles
Oil, as needed, for deep-frying

Marinade:
1 garlic clove, minced
1-inch piece of ginger, peeled and minced
  (1 tablespoon)
2 tablespoons sesame oil
$1/4$ cup soy sauce
1 stalk lemon grass, bruised
$1/4$ cup fresh orange juice

2 Japanese eggplants, cut lengthwise into quarters
1 red bell pepper, sliced lengthwise into $1/2$-inch strips
1 yellow bell pepper, sliced lengthwise into $1/2$-inch strips
8 scallions, chopped
2 baby bok choy, separated into leaves

Garnish:
Fried soba noodles
2 tablespoons toasted sesame seeds

To make the garnish:
Boil $1/8$ of the soba noodles in salted water until al dente. Drain. Deep-fry these noodles in hot oil until crispy. Set aside.

To prepare the marinade:
Combine all of the marinade ingredients. Toss the prepared vegetables in the marinade. Marinate for 2 to 6 hours. Remove the vegetables from the marinade; grill or sauté the vegetables over medium heat until tender.

To prepare the noodles:
Following the package directions, boil the remaining soba noodles in salted water until al dente. Drain. Place the cooked noodles in a large bowl. Toss with remaining marinade. Mound the noodles in the center of each plate. Distribute the vegetables evenly over the noodles. Garnish with the fried noodles and sprinkle with the toasted sesame seeds.

✳ **CHEF'S NOTE:** To bruise the lemon grass, pound the stalk with a meat mallet or rolling pin. Toast the sesame seeds in a dry skillet over medium heat until they start to pop.

4 SERVINGS

✦ ROULADES OF CHICKEN BREAST WITH JACK CHEESE AND ROASTED RED PEPPERS

With this dish, prepare the sauce and spinach while the chicken is "resting." If desired, the spinach can be quickly steamed instead of sautéed in olive oil.

Roulades:

2 red bell peppers, roasted, peeled and seeds removed

2 yellow bell peppers, roasted, peeled and seeds removed

3 cups fresh basil leaves, washed

Salt and freshly ground black pepper, to taste

4 (whole) chicken breasts, boneless, skinned, fat removed, cut in half

8 slices Monterey Jack cheese

2 tablespoons olive oil

Sauce:

2 cups water

1 red bell pepper, seeded and chopped

2 red onions, peeled and chopped

Salt and freshly ground black pepper, to taste

Spinach:

1 pound fresh spinach, washed with stems removed

1 tablespoon olive oil

Salt and freshly ground black pepper, to taste

To prepare the roulades:

Preheat oven to 350 degrees.

Cut the roasted peppers and basil into julienne strips. Season lightly with salt and pepper.

Flatten the chicken breasts and place pepper mixture in the middle of each breast. Place 1 slice of cheese on top of the filling. Roll up the chicken breasts to make the roulades. Wrap tightly with plastic wrap, tying the ends with string or excess plastic wrap. Refrigerate for 30 minutes.

Carefully unwrap the roulades. In a large sauté pan, heat the oil until it reaches the smoking point. Sauté the chicken breasts, on all sides, until lightly brown, starting with the seam-side down. Place the chicken breasts on a baking sheet and bake in the oven until a meat thermometer registers 165 degrees. Remove the chicken breasts from the oven. Cover with aluminum foil and allow to rest 10 minutes.

To make the sauce:

In a saucepan, bring the water to a boil. Add the pepper and onion; reduce to a simmer and cook until tender, about 10 minutes. Transfer the water, pepper and onion to a blender or food processor and puree until smooth. Season with salt and pepper. Keep warm.

To prepare the spinach:

In a large skillet, heat the olive oil. Sauté the spinach for 2 to 3 minutes, or until wilted. Season with salt and pepper.

Place the spinach in the center of a serving plate. Cut the chicken roulades at an angle in half or into 5 or 6 slices and arrange them on top of the spinach. Spoon a little of the sauce around the outside of the spinach.

8 SERVINGS

→ SPICY RED PEPPER SHRIMP

These tangy and spicy shrimp make a great appetizer or can be a main course when served with a flavorful steamed white rice such as jasmine or basmati and some crisp-tender sauteed snap peas.

3 tablespoons hot pepper sauce

1 cup beer

1 tablespoon red pepper seeds

2 pounds 16/20 shrimp, peeled and deveined

1 cup ketchup or tomato sauce

4 tablespoons salad oil

2 tablespoons hot pepper sauce

1 tablespoon soy sauce

1 tablespoon balsamic vinegar

1 teaspoon minced fresh ginger

2 garlic cloves, minced

To marinate the shrimp:

In a large bowl, combine the 3 tablespoons hot pepper sauce, beer and red pepper seeds. Mix well. Add the shrimp. Refrigerate overnight.

To grill the shrimp:

Prepare the grill for medium-high heat.

In a medium-size bowl, combine the ketchup, salad oil, 2 tablespoons hot pepper sauce, soy sauce, balsamic vinegar, ginger and garlic to make a basting sauce.

Remove the shrimp from the marinade and place on metal skewers. Place the skewered shrimp on the grill. Reduce heat to medium, if using a gas grill. Baste the shrimp as they cook for 4 to 5 minutes, turning them often. Serve the remaining basting sauce with the shrimp for dipping. Serve at once.

✳ **CHEF'S NOTE:** The best size shrimp to use in this dish is what chefs call 16/20 shrimp, or shrimp that come 16 to 20 pieces to a pound. For larger servings imply use larger shrimp.

8 SERVINGS AS A FIRST COURSE
4 SERVINGS AS A MAIN COURSE

⇥ ROASTED EGGPLANT NAPOLEON WITH PLUM TOMATO VINAIGRETTE

This is a great "make ahead" dish. The vinaigrette can be made three days in advance, and the napoleons themselves can be made a day ahead and reheated when needed.

1 large eggplant, cut into ¹/₂-inch slices

1 zucchini, cut into ¹/₂-inch slices

1 yellow squash, cut into ¹/₂-inch slices

1 red onion peeled, cut into ¹/₂-inch slices

2 red bell peppers cut in ¹/₂ lengthwise

Olive oil, as needed

Salt and freshly ground black pepper, to taste

4 ounces fresh mozzarella cheese cut into ¹/₄-inch slices

Vinaigrette:

4 plum tomatoes, cut in half

¹/₄ cup olive oil

2 tablespoons white wine vinegar

Salt and freshly ground black pepper, to taste

Garnish: ¹/₂ cup chopped parsley

To make the napoleons (may be made 1 day in advance):
Preheat oven to 350 degrees.

Place all the vegetables on a cookie sheet. Drizzle with olive oil. Season with salt and pepper. Roast in oven until lightly browned.

Assemble 4 napoleons starting with the roasted eggplant. Alternate colors by placing fresh mozzarella cheese in-between the slices of eggplant. Reheat the napoleons in the oven until warm, about 10 minutes.

To make the vinaigrette (may be made 3 days in advance):
Roast the tomatoes in a 400-degree oven until wilted and lightly colored. Place the roasted tomatoes in a food processor or blender and puree. If desired, strain into a saucepan. Cook over medium heat until liquid is reduced by half. Refrigerate.

Just before serving, place the tomato reduction in a mixing bowl.

Whisk in the olive oil slowly. Add the vinegar, salt and pepper.

To serve the napoleons:
Place each napoleon on a serving plate. Drizzle with the vinaigrette. Garnish each plate with a sprinkle of chopped parsley.

4 SERVINGS

⤳ WARM BROWN RICE SALAD WITH CITRUS VINAIGRETTE

Brown rice is the entire grain with only the inedible outer husk removed. The nutritious, high-fiber bran coating gives it a light tan color, nutlike flavor and chewy texture. This salad makes a great luncheon main course or is a nice side dish with simple grilled chicken or fish.

Roasted Cherry Tomatoes:

1 tablespoon olive oil

1 garlic clove, minced

2 tablespoons chopped Italian parsley

1 cup cherry tomatoes

Vinaigrette:

Zest and juice from 1 orange

Zest and juice from 1 lime

1 garlic clove, minced

6 tablespoons white wine vinegar

$^1/_2$ cup extra virgin olive oil

Sea salt, to taste

Fresh thyme leaves

$^1/_4$ cup chopped walnuts

1 cup cooked brown rice

2 scallions, sliced

$^1/_2$ red pepper, diced small

Salt and freshly ground pepper, to taste

1 can mandarin oranges, drained

$^1/_4$ pound green beans, steamed

Roasting the tomatoes:

Preheat oven to 350 degrees.

In a small oven-proof dish, combine the olive oil, garlic and parsley on small pan. Toss the cherry tomatoes in the mixture. Place the tomatoes in the oven for 5 minutes.

Making the vinaigrette:

In a small bowl, whisk all of the ingredients together.

Toasting the walnuts:

In a dry skillet, toast the chopped walnuts over medium heat for 5 minutes.

Assembling the dish:

In a large mixing bowl, fluff the rice with a fork. Add $^3/_4$ of the vinaigrette, the scallions and red peppers. Season with salt and pepper. Mound on a serving plate. Garnish with the roasted tomatoes, toasted walnuts, orange sections and steamed green beans. Drizzle with remaining vinaigrette.

4 SERVINGS

→ HERB GRILLED PORK TENDERLOIN WITH GRILLED WILD MUSHROOMS, FENNEL AND WILD GREENS

The grill is put to good use in this recipe. While the herbed pork tenderloin is grilling on one side of the grill, the other side is used to cook the wild mushrooms and fennel. It is essential that the pork marinate in the refrigerator for at least 4 hours.

Herb Grilled Pork Tenderloin:

2 pork tenderloins, about 1 pound each, trimmed of fat and silver skin

1 tablespoon chopped fresh thyme

1 tablespoon chopped fresh basil

1 tablespoon chopped garlic

2 tablespoons olive oil

Salt and freshly ground black pepper, to taste

1 large bunch fresh thyme, for grilling

Vegetables:

1 fennel bulb

4 ounces shiitake mushrooms, stems removed

4 ounces chanterelle mushrooms

4 ounces portabello mushrooms

4 ounces oyster mushrooms, left in clusters

1 head radicchio, cut in half through the core

1/2 cup olive oil

1/4 pound wild greens

Lemon Vinaigrette:

2 lemons

1 large shallot, chopped

1 cup extra virgin olive oil

Salt and freshly ground black pepper, to taste

Garnish:

White truffle oil, as needed

Grated Parmigiano-Reggiano, as needed

To grill the pork:

Make a paste with the chopped herbs, garlic and 2 tablespoons olive oil. Rub the mixture evenly over the pork. Place the pork in a glass baking dish or casserole. Cover with a lid or plastic wrap, and marinate in the refrigerator for 4 to 6 hours.

Prepare the grill for direct cooking.

Remove the pork from the refrigerator. Season the pork with salt and pepper.

Place half of the fresh thyme directly on the grill grates and lay the pork over the thyme. Allow the pork to cook over direct heat for 5 minutes, or until the meat begins to turn a golden brown.

Lift the pork from the grill and lay the remainder of the thyme on the grill. Lay the pork down on its uncooked side on the thyme. Continue grilling the pork for another 5 minutes, or until an instant-read thermometer registers 145 degrees when inserted into the thickest part of the pork tenderloin.

Remove the pork from the grill. Its internal temperature should be 160 degrees. Allow the pork to rest, covered, on a serving platter.

To prepare the vegetables:

While the pork is grilling, slice the fennel bulb into thirds. Blanch in boiling salted water and shock in ice water.

Brush the fennel, mushrooms and radicchio with the 1/2 cup olive oil. Season the vegetables with salt and pepper. Grill over direct heat for 3 to 4 minutes per side. The fennel should be nicely caramelized, the mushrooms should be golden, and radicchio just wilted. Remove the vegetables from the grill and keep warm.

To make the lemon vinaigrette:

Remove the zest from the lemons, and place the zest in a bowl. Cut the lemons in half and grill them over direct heat until caramelized, about 4 minutes. Add the shallots to the bowl. Squeeze the juice from the grilled lemons into the bowl. Stir in the extra virgin olive oil. Season to taste with salt and pepper.

To serve the pork tenderloin and vegetables: Cut the vegetables into pieces and mix with the wild greens. Dress the vegetables and wild greens with the vinaigrette. Place equal portions of the vegetables and wild greens on each serving plate. Slice the pork and arrange the pork around the vegetables and wild greens. Drizzle with more dressing. Garnish with truffle oil and cheese.

6 SERVINGS

⇨ HORSERADISH-CRUSTED ATLANTIC SALMON WITH BRAISED LENTILS AND CARAMELIZED CARROT SAUCE

Sensational tastes abound in this salmon dish, from the horseradish crust to the flavorful lentils to the unusual carrot sauce.

Lentils:

½ pound apple-smoked bacon, diced

½ cup diced celery

¾ cup diced onions

½ cup diced carrots

2 teaspoons chopped garlic

1 sprig fresh thyme

2 bay leaves

1 cup green lentils

2 quarts chicken stock

Carrot Sauce:

1 cup diced carrots

2 tablespoons olive oil

2 cups chicken stock

Horseradish Crust:

3 cups panko-style (Japanese) breadcrumbs*

¼ cup prepared horseradish

1 cup melted butter

Salmon:

4 (6-ounce) Atlantic salmon fillets

¼ cup olive oil

Salt and freshly ground black pepper, to taste

*Available in Asian markets

To braise the lentils:

Cook the bacon in a saucepan. When bacon is crisp, remove the bits and set aside. Add the celery, onions and carrots to the pan. Sauté for 5 minutes. Add the garlic and herbs. Sauté for 2 minutes. Add the lentils and stock. Bring to a boil. Reduce heat and simmer until lentils are tender, about 1 hour.

To make the carrot sauce:

Sauté the diced carrots in the oil until caramelized. Add the chicken stock and reduce by two-thirds. This will take about 30 minutes.

To make the horseradish crust:

Combine the panko breadcrumbs, horseradish and butter. Mix well.

To grill the salmon:

Prepare the grill for direct cooking.

Brush the fish with olive oil. Season the fish with salt and pepper.

Place the fish on the grill flesh side down over direct heat for 3 minutes. Turn the fish over and coat with the horseradish crust. Continue cooking for another 5 minutes.

Arrange the lentils in the center of each serving plate. Place the salmon on top of the lentils. Drizzle the carrot sauce around the fish and lentils. Garnish with the reserved bacon bits.

4 SERVINGS

✦ LEMON CURD TARTS WITH SUMMER BERRIES AND RASPBERRY COULIS

Lemon curd is traditionally a high-fat, high-cholesterol dessert. This lower-fat recipe uses whole eggs rather than egg yolks and cuts back on the usual amount of butter.

Tart Shells:
3 sheets phyllo dough
Granulated sugar, as needed

Lemon Curd:
1 and 1/2 cups granulated sugar
3 tablespoons fine lemon zest
4 large eggs
1 and 1/2 cups fresh lemon juice (from 6 lemons)
4 tablespoons butter

Raspberry Coulis:
2 pints fresh raspberries
2 tablespoons granulated sugar
1 tablespoon Grand Marnier (orange-flavored liqueur)

Garnish:
Assorted summer berries (blackberries, raspberries and blueberries)
Confectioners' sugar, as needed

To make the tart shells:
Preheat oven to 350 degrees.

Cut the sheets of phyllo dough into 18 (5x5-inch) squares. Place 1 square of dough on a clean work surface. Spray the dough with non-stick cooking spray, and sprinkle lightly with sugar. Repeat this process using 3 squares of dough for each tart shell.

Using a standard-size muffin pan, place the 3 squares of dough into each compartment, shaping to fit. Press the dough into the bottom and up the sides of each compartment. Bake until golden brown, 8 to 12 minutes. Watch the tart shells carefully so they do not burn. Set aside to cool.

To make the lemon curd:
In a heavy saucepan over medium heat, combine the sugar, zest and egg, stirring constantly. After the sugar is dissolved and the mixture reaches the nappe stage (it should coat the back of a spoon), remove from the heat.

Pour the mixture into a bowl, add the butter, and stir until the butter is completely melted. Allow to cool for 10 to 15 minutes. Then pour 1/4 cup of the lemon curd into each tart shell. The tart shells are very delicate so handle with care. Set aside.

To make the raspberry coulis:
Place the berries, sugar and liqueur in a food processor. Process until smooth. Press the mixture through a sieve or cheesecloth to remove seeds. Refrigerate.

To assemble:
Place a lemon curd tart on a plate. Drizzle raspberry coulis around the tart. Top with assorted summer berries. Dust with confectioner's sugar.

Variations:

Top each tart with meringue and brown under a broiler or with a small blowtorch. Sprinkle berries around each tart.

Top each tart with fat-free frozen vanilla bean yogurt available in supermarkets. Sprinkle berries around each tart.

CHEF'S NOTE: To make a large amount of lemon zest, use a vegetable peeler to remove the zest from the lemons, then place the zest in a food processor to mince it.

8 TO 10 SERVINGS

⇥ PAVLOVA WITH RASPBERRY SAUCE

Originating in Australia, pavlova is a famous dessert named after the Russian ballerina Anna Pavlova. It consists of a crisp meringue topped with whipped cream and fruit. In this version, the meringue is topped with a light pastry cream and fresh berries.

Meringue Shells:
4 large egg whites
1 cup granulated sugar

Light Pastry Cream:
2 cups non-fat milk
1 cup granulated sugar
Pinch of salt
3 tablespoons cornstarch
1 tablespoon cake flour
1 large egg yolk
2 large whole eggs
1 teaspoon vanilla extract
2 tablespoons unsalted butter

Raspberry Sauce:
1 pint fresh raspberries
3 tablespoons granulated sugar
1 tablespoon lemon juice
3 tablespoons water

Fresh berries (blackberries, blueberries, raspberries, strawberries), as needed

To make the meringue shells:
Preheat oven to 225 degrees.

In a stainless steel bowl, whip the egg whites using a hand mixer. Slowly add the sugar and continue whipping until stiff peaks form. Spoon the whites onto a waxed paper or parchment-lined sheet pan using 3 heaping tablespoons of whites per shell (make 6 to 8 shells). With the backside of a teaspoon, make a well in the center of each shell, deep and wide enough to fill with cream and top with fruit.

Place the shells in the warm oven for 2 hours to dry. Remove the shells from the oven and store in an airtight container.

To make the light pastry cream:
In a saucepan, bring 1 and $1/2$ cups of milk, $1/2$ cup of sugar and salt to a boil.

In a mixing bowl, combine the cornstarch, flour and remaining sugar; slowly add the remaining milk to form a smooth paste. Add the egg yolk and whole eggs to the cornstarch mixture. Combine well. Temper the cornstarch mixture and add to boiling milk. Bring the mixture back to a second boil, constantly stirring; cook for 3 minutes.

Remove from heat; stir in vanilla extract and butter. Whisk well. Pour into a large rectangular pan. Cover with buttered sheets of waxed paper to prevent a skin from forming on the pastry cream. Refrigerate.

To make the raspberry sauce:
In a saucepan, combine all sauce ingredients. Cook berries until they break down and then bring mixture to a boil for 1 minute. Strain sauce through a sieve to remove seeds. Chill.

To assemble the pavlova:
Fill the meringue shells with cold pastry cream and top with fresh fruit. Spoon the raspberry sauce around the shells and serve immediately.

✳ **CHEF'S NOTE:** Tempering means raising the temperature of a cold liquid gradually by slowly adding a hot liquid to it and stirring.

6 TO 8 SERVINGS

→ INDEX

☀ ABOUT THE UNIVERSITY AND "MASTER CLASS AT JOHNSON & WALES"

Johnson & Wales University – America's Career University" is a private, non-profit educational institution with campuses in Providence, Rhode Island; Norfolk, Virginia; Charleston, South Carolina; North Miami, Florida and Denver Colorado. With associate and bachelor's degree programs in our College of Culinary Arts in culinary arts, baking and pastry arts, and culinary nutrition, as well as foodservice management degrees housed in The Hospitality College, we are the world's largest foodservice educator.

When Johnson & Wales first opened its doors in 1914, with "two students and one typewriter" its founders, Gertrude Johnson and Mary Wales never envisioned the Johnson & Wales University of today – with over 13,500 students from all 50 states and over 90 countries studying at five domestic campuses and educational partners around the globe, earning both undergraduate and graduate degrees. They had no idea that 59 years later the University would open a world-class College of Culinary Arts, dedicated to continuing the University's longstanding tradition of preparing our students for important careers in critical industry segments, and destined to become the world's largest foodservice educator. This college complements The Hospitality College and the College of Business, which, along with our School of Technology prepare career-ready graduates, 98% of whom are employed in their chosen field within 60 days of graduation. We are proud to have maintained this record for well over 20 years.

Our focus, as America's Career University®, has always been on our students and the relationship with employers that continues to help us develop the most up-to-date and relevant curriculum. Students study in their majors from the beginning of their freshman year, and also begin to prepare for their job search from day one. Hands-on learning is a mainstay of our educational mission, resulting in internship and cooperative education opportunities for students in all majors, with the majority of programs requiring at least one term of practical work experience. Whether in culinary arts, hotel management or accounting, the classes are small, the instructors have industry experience, and the top employers in the field have worked with us to ensure that what is taught in the classroom has relevance in the real world.

What is taught to our students at each of our campus locations prepares them with an educational experience second-to-none. And now, for the first time, we are bringing the opportunity to participate with our chefs and students to food lovers across the nation, through the public television series "Master Class at Johnson & Wales" and this, the first companion cookbook. The show has been an incredible culinary journey, in more ways than one, and truly is a labor of love. "Master Class at Johnson & Wales" is an extension of our commitment to providing the highest quality educational experience – this time outside the campus confines.

America's Career University®

Text © 2002 by Johnson & Wales University
Photography © 2002 by Marjorie Poore Productions
Design © 2002 by Marjorie Poore Productions

Editor: Linda Beaulieu

MPP Books
363 14th Avenue,
San Francisco, California 94118
Printed In Korea

Cuisinart is proud to sponsor
Public Broadcasting's
"Master Class at Johnson & Wales".
When Cuisinart introduced home cooks
to the world-famous food processor,
we shared a secret professional
cooks had known for years.
Today, we continue to strive for
culinary excellence, and this is why
we are pleased to be part of
"Master Class at Johnson & Wales".

Cuisinart

Cuisinart® Premier Series Food Processors

The next generation Cuisinart food processor offers sleek, contemporary looks and more food prep options than ever! The Premier Series is *smooth* – all curves, with wipe-clean solid state touchpads. These new models feature a separate dough control that automatically adjusts the motor to the right speed for kneading, and a specially designed metal dough blade to make the process perfect. With one-piece, extra large feed tubes, dishwasher safe parts, and a variety of shredding and slicing discs, Cuisinart food processors – Premier Series or Classic – remain the ultimate food prep tool.

SmartStick® Extendable Hand Blender

Leave it to Cuisinart to extend your blending options! Our SmartStick® Extendable Shaft Hand Blender features an adjustable shaft that easily extends to reach deep into big pots of soup and sauces and into the very bottom of tall pitchers. Four speeds, plus our handy Mini-Prep™ chopper/grinder, a whipping disc and a chopping blade, further extend your food prep options.

SmartPower™ CountUp™ 9-Speed Electronic Hand Mixer

This is the mixer you can count on. Literally! A digital timer, built right into an exceptionally comfortable handle, starts running the instant you start mixing. You'll never over – or under – mix again. With 220 watts, automatic feedback power that kicks in when needed, 9 speeds (including 3 extra low and a really Smooth Start™), plus a chef's whisk, you'll find there's very little this mixer can't handle!

SmartPower™ 7-Speed Electronic Blender

This SmartPower™ sets a new standard in blending. A powerful motor is strong enough to crush ice without liquid, yet precise enough to mince delicate herbs. The 40-ounce glass jar with dripless spout holds enough drinks, salsa or soup for a crowd. Easy-to-clean touchpad, pulse control, one-touch ice crushing, and a design chosen as the best by consumers, make this blender a very smart choice.

Custom Control™ Total Touch® Toaster

Smooth lines and user-friendly features make this premium Cuisinart toaster a perfect fit for every lifestyle. It toasts everything from whole bagels to the thinnest breads and looks good while doing it! Perfect toast is guaranteed with special settings like 1-Slice Single Select and Bagel Buttons, as well as Defrost and Reheat controls. And Your Choice™ Browning Memory will remember just how you like it!

Brew Central™ 12-Cup Programmable Coffeemaker

The Cuisinart® Brew Central™ Coffeemaker brings a revolutionary new look to coffee. The perfect blend of vintage and hi tech, it wraps top coffeemaking technology in smooth curves and elegant brushed stainless steel. This ultimate coffeemaker is fully programmable, and features an easy to read digital clock set into a graceful ellipse that makes setting start and stop times simple. Filters for both water and coffee ensure the purest, just brewed flavor, and a heater plate with a built-in sensor keeps coffee at a perfect temperature. Coffee is always fresh, hot, and ready when you are, with the Brew Central™ Coffeemaker, from Cuisinart.

Cuisinart

Cuisinart® countertop appliances are designed to be versatile and easy to use. They reduce the time you spend on the mundane tasks of food preparation, allowing you the freedom to be a little more creative in the kitchen.

Crafted from the finest quality materials, each product reflects Cuisinart's commitment to quality, innovation and performance. From our One and Only original Food Processor, to our toasters, blenders, mixers and coffeemakers, Cuisinart® products stand ready to offer you years of service.

Enjoy your time with us. We think you will find it absolutely delicious!

Cuisinart

Over 25 years ago, Cuisinart established a new standard in professional cookware. Today we offer three distinctive lines, each including a full range of basic and specialty pieces, to suit every style of cooking.

Cuisinart uses only the finest professional quality materials in the construction of our cookware. Designed from the inside out for today's healthy, relaxed lifestyles, all three lines bring together the beauty of functionality and the pleasure of presentation.

From stovetop to oven to tabletop, Cuisinart® cookware makes cooking a pleasure.

Cuisinart® Copper Classic™ Cookware

This premium line of Cuisinart cookware is a superb example of traditional craftsmanship. Constructed of the finest materials for cooking, triple-ply Copper Classic Cookware bonds brilliant copper, pure aluminum and mirror-finish stainless steel for unsurpassed looks, durability and performance. Take it from stovetop to oven to table, and Savor the Good Life™.

Cuisinart® MultiClad Stainless Cookware

Cuisinart honors a 30+ year commitment to producing only top-quality, innovative cookware with the MultiClad Stainless collection. The triple-ply construction combines the highest grade stainless steel and pure, solid aluminum to create a line of cookware that perfectly performs all of the classic cooking techniques. The look is sensational. Smooth, brushed stainless steel exteriors. Mirror-finish, naturally stick-free stainless cooking surfaces. And sandwiched between, a pure aluminum core that extends across the bottoms and up the sides for unparalleled heat conduction. Tightfitting lids seal in flavor and nutrients for results that are consistently delicious.

Cuisinart® Stick Free Stainless Non-Stick Cookware

Cuisinart has combined nonstick convenience with professional quality cookware, setting a new standard in nonstick cookware. It contains no aluminum and is designed for flavorful, healthful cooking. Through a special Excalibur® Multi-Layer System, stainless steel is actually built into the nonstick material for superior durability.

NOTES

NOTES

NOTES

NOTES

NOTES

NOTES